KETO COOKING
FOR BEGINNERS!

Easy recipes and essential
information for living KETO

Publications International, Ltd.

CONTENTS

INTRODUCTION TO KETO

The purpose of this book is to help educate you about the types of dietary and blood fats and their contribution to health, and their relation to ketones and the ketogenic diet. It provides you with recipes that focus on healthy fats, proteins and non-starchy vegetables and de-emphasizes carbohydrates—particularly those that are refined or processed.

Your healthcare provider may help you determine if these approaches to eating and dieting are appropriate for you, so ask your doctor before you begin this or any other diet program.

DIETARY FATS AND OILS, WEIGHT AND HEALTH

Want to hear some good news about dietary fats and oils—especially how they relate to weight and health?

Consuming dietary fats and oils is not as bad as you might think—nor will consuming dietary fats and oils necessarily make you fat. The right amounts and types of dietary fats and oils may actually be satisfying and contribute to weight loss and weight maintenance. Dietary fats and oils are essential to your overall diet. Understanding what dietary fats and oils are and how they fit into an overall diet will help you with food selection, preparation and meal and menu planning.

The keto diet is based on ketones, organic compounds that are produced when dietary carbohydrates are limited. Ketosis is a normal metabolic process whereby the body burns stored fats instead of glucose from carbohydrates for energy. A diet based on ketosis, with its abundance of dietary fats and oils may actually help your dieting efforts. Understanding more about ketones and their place in a ketogenic diet may assist your food choices and dietary efforts.

In addition to their role in weight loss and weight management, different types of dietary fats and oils and ketones are important for brain function, some disease protection and management, and overall health if used advantageously and correctly.

Dietary fats and oils are naturally found in foods and beverages such as dairy products, eggs, nuts, meats and seeds. Manufactured dietary fats and oils are found in some beverages, processed foods like margarine, cheeses and meats. Ketones are produced by the human body—you'll soon discover how.

There are differing viewpoints on the benefits of different types of dietary fats and oils and about ketones, the ideal amounts to consume and how ketones may sensibly be used for weight loss.

TYPES OF FATS

Saturated fats are primarily found in foods from animal sources, such as meat, poultry and full-fat dairy products, while trans fats are mostly created when oils are partially hydrogenated to improve their cooking applications and to give them a longer shelf life. Saturated and trans fats may place a person at greater risk for heart disease. On the other hand, unsaturated fats that include monounsaturated and polyunsaturated fatty acids, found in plant-based foods such as avocados, nuts and seeds and olives and olive oil, and in fatty fish such as salmon, sardines and tuna tend to lower the risk of heart issues.

The American Heart Association (AHA) Diet and Lifestyle Recommendations suggest that a person limit saturated and trans fats and replace them with monounsaturated and polyunsaturated fats. If blood cholesterol needs to be lowered, then the recommendation is to reduce saturated fat to no more than 5 to 6 percent of total calories. For someone consuming 2,000 calories a day, this is about 13 grams of saturated fat, or about 117 calories. This is the equivalent of about 1 ounce of Cheddar cheese (9.4% total fat with 6 grams of saturated fat) and about 3 ounces of regular ground beef (25% total fat with 6.1 grams of saturated fat).

Try to eliminate trans fats (fats that have been processed into saturated fats) completely, or limit them to less than 1 percent of total daily calories. On a 2,000-calorie diet, this means that fewer than 20 calories (about 2 grams) should be derived from trans fats.

In contrast, in the ketogenic diet as much as 75 percent of daily calories are derived from fat; up to 30 percent of daily calories are to come from proteins and no more than 10 percent of daily calories are to come from carbohydrates (about 20 to 50 grams).

CHOOSE THE RIGHT FATS

Fats are essential for proper body functioning and contribute satisfaction to diets, plus fats add flavor to foods and beverages. Still, fats provide more than twice the number of calories as carbohydrates or proteins (9 calories per gram compared to 4 calories per gram respectively). On a ketogenic diet, there is a different approach to fats than other diets that may restrict fats. The key is to understand the importance of fats in ketogenic diets and how to use them to your advantage.

WHAT'S INSIDE FATS AND OILS?

Fats and oils are composed of fatty acids that contain different properties. Some fatty acids are considered unhealthy and may contribute to certain diseases, while other fatty acids are considered to be healthier and may be better for weight loss and weight maintenance in the long run.

The main types of fatty acids that are found in our food supply include saturated fatty acids, monounsaturated fatty acids, polyunsaturated fatty acids, trans fatty acids, omega-3 and omega-6 fatty acids and triglycerides. Cholesterol is a waxy substance that is found in some foods and beverages and is also produced by the body.

SATURATED FATTY ACIDS (OR SATURATED FATS) are solid at room temperature. They are fully saturated or packed with fatty acids. (The name refers to its chemical makeup; saturated fats are short-chain fats with no double bonds and are "saturated" or filled with hydrogen.) They are a hard type of fat for the body to break down and may increase the risk for heart disease and stroke.

Saturated fats are mostly found in animal foods such as dairy products, lard and meats and in some tropical oils including coconut, palm and palm kernel oil. By consuming a mixture of foods and beverages that are higher in saturated fatty acids, monounsaturated fatty acids and omega-3 fatty acids, blood cholesterol levels may be lowered and blood profiles may improve. An active lifestyle is also a contributing factor in improved lipid profiles.

MONOUNSATURATED FATTY ACIDS (OR MONOUNSATURATED FATS) are liquid or soft at room temperature. They have one space or opening within their chain of fatty acids, which makes it easier for the body to metabolize or break down. Partly for this reason, monounsaturated fats are considered to be healthier than saturated fats. Also, monounsaturated fats may help to lower blood cholesterol and decrease the risk of heart disease, so they are considered to be "heart-healthy".

Monounsaturated fats are found in avocados, canola oil, olives and nuts and their respective oils, seeds, and safflower and sunflower oils. They are more fragile than saturated fatty acids and may break down with exposure to air or heat.

POLYUNSATURATED FATTY ACIDS (OR POLYUNSATURATED FATS) may also be liquid or soft at room temperature, but they may solidify when chilled. Polyunsaturated fats have many spaces or openings within their chain of fatty acids, which makes them much easier for the body to process (and to breakdown with exposure to air or heat).

Polyunsaturated fats provide nutrients for the development and maintenance of healthy body cells, which include vitamin E, an important antioxidant that protects the cells from damage. Polyunsaturated fats may also help to reduce blood cholesterol and lower the risk of heart disease and stroke when they

are consumed in moderation and when they replace saturated and trans fats in the diet. Daily fat consumption should be comprised mostly of monounsaturated or polyunsaturated fats.

Oils with polyunsaturated fats include corn, olive, soybean and sunflower oils. Polyunsaturated fats may also be found in fatty fish including herring, mackerel, salmon and trout, along with other seafood, nuts and seeds. By reducing highly processed carbohydrate-containing foods in the diet, some polyunsaturated fats will be reduced, but those from healthier food sources should remain.

TRANS FATTY ACIDS (OR TRANS FATS) are fatty acids that have been processed into saturated fats. Trans fats are created by industrial methods through the process of hydrogenation, which solidifies or partially solidifies liquid vegetable oils. Trans fats, difficult for the body to process and eliminate, trigger inflammation. Consequently, trans fats are implicated in cardiovascular disease, diabetes, insulin resistance, metabolic disease and stroke.

Trans fats are commonly found in many fried foods and baked goods such as crackers, cookies, chips, French fries, pastries, pie crust and pizza dough. They also naturally occur in small amounts in some dairy products and meats.

The terms "hydrogenated" and "partially hydrogenated oils" on the Nutrition Facts Panel used to mean that foods and beverages contained trans fats. In 2015, the U.S. Food and Drug Administration (FDA) determined that partially hydrogenated oils (the primary dietary source of artificial trans fats in processed foods) are "generally not recognized as safe in human food." Food manufacturers were given 3 years (until 2018) to comply with removing all trans fats from food.

Inspect nutrition labels to make sure you're avoiding all trans fats. Even if a food package states "0 grams of trans fats," it might still contain some trans fats if the amount per serving is less than 0.5 grams, so check the ingredients to make sure there are no hydrogenated or partially hydrogenated oils listed.

Omega-3 and **Omega-6 Fatty Acids** are both types of polyunsaturated fats with unique properties.

OMEGA-3 FATTY ACIDS (OR OMEGA-3 FATS) are essential fats, which means that they must be supplied by the diet for healthy body functioning. Omega-3 fats, particularly EPA and DHA, are beneficial to the heart. They may decrease arrhythmias (abnormal heartbeats) and triglycerides stored in fat cells, increase tissue flexibility, improve cholesterol profiles, lower blood pressure, reduce inflammation and slow the growth of plaque in the arteries. (Plaque is a hard substance that is composed of cholesterol, calcium and clotting materials.)

Omega-3 fats may also help to relieve the symptoms of chronic diseases such as arthritis, depression and dementia. EPA and DHA are components of hormones that regulate immune function, and DHA is vital for brain development and cognition.

Good sources of omega-3 fats include seafood such as mackerel, sardines, salmon, tuna and shellfish and plant sources like canola and soybean oils, flaxseed and walnuts.

OMEGA-6 FATTY ACIDS (OR OMEGA-6 FATS) are also polyunsaturated fats and essential fatty acids. Omega-6 fats perform vital roles in brain function, normal development and growth. They also help maintain reproduction, regulate metabolism and support healthy skin and hair and bone health. However, omega-6 fatty acids may promote inflammation and contribute to complex regional pain syndrome. Chronic inflammation may contribute to asthma, autoimmunity and neurodegenerative diseases, cancers and coronary heart disease.

Omega-6 fats are prevalent in eggs, meats, poultry, salad dressings and corn, grape seed and sunflower oils. Linoleic acid (LA) is found in corn, cottonseed, safflower, soybean and sunflower oils among other oils. Arachidonic acid (AA) is found in small amounts in eggs, meats and poultry. LA can be converted to AA in the body. Omega-6 fats are often used in fried and processed foods, so a diet that is filled with highly processed foods may be disproportionately high in omega-6 fatty acids.

A healthy diet contains a balance of omega-3 and omega-6 fatty acids (or a ratio of 1:1), although the typical American diet tends to contain more omega-6 fatty acids than omega-3 fatty acids. Consuming more omega-3 fats through food sources, such as fish and chia or flax seeds, may help to balance this pattern.

CHOLESTEROL is an essential component in the cell membranes of brain and nerve cells and for hormone formation. It is used to maintain brain health for memory formation and for the production of hormones and vitamin D. When your skin absorbs sunlight, cholesterol within the cells is converted to vitamin D.

Cholesterol is a waxy substance that is found in animal foods such as dairy products, eggs and meats. The body produces cholesterol on its own from saturated fat or glucose so it is not needed from food.

Common thought used to be that a high level of dietary cholesterol contributed to coronary heart disease, diabetes, stroke or peripheral vascular disease. This is because excess cholesterol may form plaque between the layers of the artery walls. In turn, plaque may clog arteries, reduce their flexibility, interfere with blood circulation and lead to atherosclerosis, or "hardening" of the arteries. Plaque can also break apart and lead to blood clots. If blood clots form and block narrowed arteries, then a heart attack or stroke may occur.

Current thinking focuses more on the type of dietary and blood cholesterol and the types of fatty acids that they transport, and that consuming cholesterol doesn't necessarily lead to higher blood cholesterol levels. In fact, blood cholesterol levels may actually lower on a ketogenic diet.

LDL-CHOLESTEROL is considered to be "bad" cholesterol because it may contribute to increased plaque in arteries, decrease flexibility and raise the risk of atherosclerosis (hardening of the arteries). Excess calories, dietary cholesterol, saturated fat, trans fats and total fat in the diet are some of the dietary factors that may increase LDL-cholesterol. Lifestyle factors and genetics that may also increase LDL-cholesterol include age, diabetes, family history, high blood pressure, male gender, obesity and physical inactivity. A healthy range of LDL-cholesterol is considered to be 100-129 mg/dL. Carbohydrate consumption from refined carbohydrates that are high in sugar and low in fiber is associated with higher levels of LDL-cholesterol and triglycerides. There is some thought that the size of LDL-particles are more important. Small and dense LDL particles may conveniently lodge in artery walls, cause inflammation and lead to heart disease.

HDL-CHOLESTEROL is considered to be "good" cholesterol because it helps remove cholesterol from the arteries and transport it back to the liver where it is broken down and excreted from the body. A healthy level of HDL-cholesterol (60 mg/dL or higher) may also protect against heart attack and stroke, while a low level of HDL-cholesterol (less than 40 mg/dL) may increase the risk of heart disease.

The protective benefits of HDL-cholesterol may depend upon the levels of other blood fats that are associated with coronary heart disease. For example, if LDL-cholesterol is not within normal range or if most LDL-cholesterol particles are small, even a high HDL-cholesterol level may not be protective.

Fish and soy foods, rich in mono and polyunsaturated fatty acids (MUFAs and PUFAs) may increase HDL-cholesterol, Consuming foods that are high in fiber and antioxidants from permissible ketogenic fruits and vegetables may help prevent LDL-cholesterol from injuring the artery walls.

THERE ARE TWO MAIN TYPES OF CHOLESTEROL

low-density lipoprotein (LDL) cholesterol
"bad" cholesterol

high-density lipoprotein (HDL) cholesterol
"good" cholesterol

TRIGLYCERIDES are the main form of fat that is found in food and within the body. Triglycerides are composed of three fatty acids that vary in composition (saturated, unsaturated or a combination). High levels of triglycerides in the blood are associated with atherosclerosis. Certain diseases (such as diabetes or heart disease) and medications, excessive alcohol consumption, high carbohydrate intake, obesity, physical inactivity, smoking and some genetic disorders may contribute to elevated blood triglycerides.

This is because elevated blood triglycerides are often associated with high blood cholesterol, high LDL-cholesterol and/or low HDL-cholesterol, which are high-risk factors that are associated with these diseases and conditions.

COMMON FAT-CONTAINING FOODS

Common fat-containing foods include (but are not limited to) avocados, beef, butter, cheese, chocolate, coconut, coconut milk and coconut oil, nuts and seeds (including chia and flax seeds), oils (including canola, olive and peanut oils), salmon, sardines and walnuts.

AVOCADOS

Avocados, technically a fruit, contain a lot of fat, but don't avoid them because of it! They contain omega-3 fatty acids, monounsaturated fatty acids, protein and fiber, as well as the B-vitamins, vitamin C, E and K, magnesium, potassium and healthy monounsaturated fatty acids. One cup of sliced avocado contains about 234 calories, 21 grams of total fat, 3.1 grams of saturated fat, 14 grams of monounsaturated fat and 2.7 grams of polyunsaturated fat with no cholesterol.

BEEF

Beef is more than burgers and steaks. There are three cuts: lean (3 grams of fat per ounce as round, sirloin and flank steak), medium-fat (5 grams of fat per ounce as rump roast, Porterhouse and T-bone) and high-fat (8 grams fat per ounce as USDA Prime, ribs and corned beef). Some cuts have polyunsaturated fats and others contain omega-3 fats and vitamins such as vitamins A and E, depending on their feed. Free-range beef might be rich in certain minerals from grazing. Beef is full of other nutrients, such as B-vitamins, choline, iron, protein, selenium and zinc and has prominence in ketogenic diets.

BUTTER AND MARGARINE

Butter has short-, medium- and long-chain fatty acids. The short-chain fatty acid is called butyric acid and the medium-chain fatty acid is called myristic acid. Both of these saturated fats have health benefits. They are relatively easy to transport and easy for the body to absorb. In comparison, stearic and palmitic acids, the longer-chain fatty acids, may be cardiovascular risk factors in higher amounts in the diet.

Margarine is an imitation butter spread that is manufactured from refined vegetable oil and water. Historically, vegetable oil was hardened in a process called hydrogenation that created unhealthy trans fats that contributed to heart disease. Trans fats have subsequently been removed from the majority of margarine products.

Margarine contains coloring, flavoring, milk solids, preservatives and sodium. The calories in margarine and butter may be similar in comparative portion sizes, but the composition of fatty acids differ. Generally, firmer margarines contain more saturated fats, while softer margarine may contain 10 to 20 percent saturated fats.

CHEESE

Cheese that is made from cow's milk contains about 69 percent saturated fatty acids, 24 percent monounsaturated fatty acids and 3 percent polyunsaturated fatty acids. Cheese that is made from goat's milk contains about 71 percent saturated fatty acids, 22 percent monounsaturated fatty acids and 3 percent polyunsaturated fatty acids. Cheddar, Swiss and Parmesan cheese are some varieties with the least total carbohydrates. Use cheese to add taste, texture and healthy fats to recipes.

CHOCOLATE

The fat that is found in cocoa plants and predominant in dark chocolate is cocoa butter, which is about 33 percent monounsaturated oleic fatty acid and 33 percent stearic fatty acid. In general, stearic fatty acids from plants, although saturated, seem to neither lower high HDL-cholesterol nor increase LDL- or total cholesterol. But on a ketogenic diet, be careful about the carbohydrates in chocolate in the forms of milk solids, sugars and others.

COCONUT, COCONUT MILK AND COCONUT OIL

Coconut, coconut milk and coconut oil are used throughout the world for their distinctive tastes and textures. They were considered unhealthy due to their saturated fat content but are now valued for their healthful properties.

About 60 percent of the saturated fats in coconut oil are in the form of medium-chain triglycerides (MCTs) that are absorbed directly by the gastrointestinal tract and metabolized immediately by the liver for energy. For this and other reasons, MCTs may be beneficial in preventing atherosclerosis. MCTs may also help to trigger ketosis and may be effective for providing energy at the start of ketogenic diets.

Natural cholesterol-free coconut oil is solid at room temperature but it turns liquid at relatively low temperatures (about 80°F). It can be substituted for cholesterol-containing butter or lard in cooking and baking. Two main types of coconut oil are refined and virgin; both are acceptable for cooking and baking, but virgin coconut oil has more of a coconut flavor than refined.

There are many liquid coconut products available; they cannot generally be used interchangeably. Their carbohydrate content may be too high to include in a ketogenic diet, so check the label. Coconut milk is made by simmering shredded coconut in water and then straining out and squeezing the coconut to extract the liquid. Coconut milk beverages may act as milk substitutes. Coconut water is the liquid from the inside of a coconut and is sold for drinking, not cooking. Coconut cream is similar to coconut milk, but is thicker because it contains less water. Often a layer of coconut cream will separate from the milk in a can of regular coconut milk. To blend it back into the milk, shake the can before opening. Or just pour the entire contents of the can into whatever you're cooking and stir well (the heat will melt the cream back into the milk). Avoid cream of coconut; this is sweetened coconut cream and it used primarily in desserts and drinks.

NUTS AND SEEDS

Nuts and seeds range in total fat, fatty acids and other nutrients. They are filled with protein, mostly mono- and polyunsaturated fatty acids and omega-3 fatty acids, insoluble fiber, the B vitamins and vitamin E and magnesium, manganese, phosphorus and zinc among other nutrients.

The fatty acids in almonds and walnuts may actually be helpful in lowering other blood fats. Almonds have been shown to help increase antioxidant vitamin E and lower blood cholesterol. Walnuts have a high percentage of omega-3 fats. Additionally, many nuts have a low Glycemic Index (GI) value, which means that they may be useful in insulin management and a good snack.

Pine nuts, common to heart-healthy Mediterranean diets, add a distinctive buttery and creamy touch to recipes. One-half cup contains about 673 calories, 10 grams of protein, 78 grams of total fat, 7 grams of saturated fat, almost 45 grams of monounsaturated fat, 24 grams of polyunsaturated fat and no cholesterol. The amount of dietary fiber ranges from 7 to 12 grams per half cup.

CHIA SEEDS

Chia seeds are tiny black seeds that contain antioxidants, calcium, carbohydrates, fats, fiber, omega-3 fatty acids and protein. Their fiber and omega-3 fat content are impressive with 11 grams of fiber per ounce (about 35 percent) and 60 percent of their total fat as ALA omega-3 fatty acids. Chia seeds are mild and nutty and add texture to foods and beverages. When mixed with water, chia seeds swell and become gel-like.

FLAX SEEDS

Similar to walnuts, flax seeds contain a significant amount of omega-3 fats such as alpha-linolenic acid (ALA): 1 tablespoon of ground flaxseed contains about 1.8 grams of omega-3 fats. Flax seeds also contain lignans with antioxidant and estrogen qualities and soluble and insoluble fibers that may offer protection against certain cancers and heart disease through their anti-inflammatory activity and heart beat normalization. Flax seeds and ground flaxseed spoil quickly so keep them in the freezer if you're not going to use them right away.

OILS

Like butter and margarine, some oils are also considered controversial—particularly the tropical oils: coconut oil, palm oil and palm kernel oil. Palm oil is an all-purpose cooking oil that is used in vegetable oil blends to impart flavor. It contains about 51 percent saturated fatty acids, 39 percent monounsaturated fatty acids and 10 percent polyunsaturated fatty acids. One tablespoon of palm oil contains about 5 grams of heart-healthy monounsaturated fatty acids.

Palm kernel oil contains about 86 percent saturated fatty acids, 12 percent monounsaturated fatty acids and 2 percent polyunsaturated fatty acids. One tablespoon of palm kernel oil contains about 3.1 grams of heart-healthy monounsaturated fatty acids. Palm kernel oil is used in commercial baking since it tends to remains stable at high temperatures and can be stored longer than some other oils.

In contrast, canola oil, olive oil and peanut oil have more favorable fatty acid profiles. Canola oil contains about 6 percent saturated fatty acids, 62 percent monounsaturated fatty acids and 32 percent polyunsaturated fatty acids. One tablespoon of canola oil contains about 9 grams of heart-healthy monounsaturated fatty acids. Canola oil is commonly used for baking, frying and in salad dressings.

Olive oil contains about 14 percent saturated fatty acids, 73 percent monounsaturated fatty acids and 11 percent polyunsaturated fatty acids. One tablespoon of olive oil contains about 10 grams of heart-healthy monounsaturated fatty acids. Virgin olive oil is used as an all-purpose cooking oil and in salad dressing. Extra virgin olive oil is primarily used to dress salads, vegetables and entrées. Light and extra-light olive oil generally have less flavor and are mainly used for sautéing and stir-frying since they withstand more heat than extra virgin olive oil.

Peanut oil contains about 18 percent saturated fatty acids, 49 percent monounsaturated fatty acids and 33 percent polyunsaturated fatty acids. One tablespoon of peanut oil contains about 6 grams of heart-healthy monounsaturated fatty acids. Peanut oil has a higher smoke point than most olive oil blends, so is useful as an all-purpose oil in cooking and frying. Peanut oil is commonly used in Asian cuisine, while olive oil is used in Mediterranean cuisine. Canola oil is an all-purpose oil used in all types of cooking.

SALMON, SARDINES AND OTHER FATTY FISH

Generally the amount of omega-3 fatty acids in cold-water fatty fish, such as Albacore tuna, anchovies, Artic char, black cod, herring, salmon, sardines, mackerel and trout is significant. The amount of omega-3s may vary according to the composition of fish that fish consume, growing conditions and locations. Farmed fish may have higher levels of EPA and DHA than wild-caught fish. These considerations may affect flavor and cost.

Wild Atlantic salmon contains about 1.22 grams of DHA and 0.35 grams of EPA per 3-ounce serving. In comparison, sardines contain about 0.74 grams of DHA and 0.45 grams of EPA per 3-ounce serving and wild rainbow trout contains about 0.44 grams of DHA and 0.40 grams of EPA per 3-ounce serving.

FAT DIGESTION, ABSORPTION, METABOLISM AND STORAGE

In general, the more solidified the fat or oil, the more challenging it is for the body to process, use, eliminate or store. Monounsaturated and polyunsaturated fatty acids that are found in avocados, nuts and plant oils are largely easier for the body to handle. Saturated fats that are found in cheese, meats and milk as well as coconuts and palm products are acceptable on a ketogenic diet if consumed in moderation. Their role in cardiovascular disease is still of concern.

Avocados, beef fat, butter, mayonnaise, nut butters, poultry skin and salad dressings have delicious mouth feel due to their unique compositions of fats and oils. From the moment these buttery, creamy and smooth foods are consumed, their complex fat digestion begins.

FAT DIGESTION

Fat digestion begins in the mouth, where it is mostly physical. The teeth tear apart fatty foods and the temperature within the mouth melts some of the fats. A gland under the tongue also secretes a fat-splitting enzyme called lipase.

Then the fatty residue passes through the esophagus into the stomach, where it mixes with gastric lipase, an enzyme that is secreted by the stomach cells. Gastric lipase continues fat digestion as the stomach muscles churn and mix the stomach contents. Together, this process continues to break down the fat by breaking up large fat molecules into smaller ones and evenly distributing them.

Most of the fats in foods and beverages are packaged in the form of triglycerides, which must be broken down into fatty acids and a molecule called glycerol for absorption. This process tends to be slow. As a result, fats tend to linger in the stomach and contribute to fullness or satiety. This can take up to a few hours and is why a fatty meal is so filling and why a low-fat meal may be so unsatisfying. One of the plusses of the ketogenic diet is a lack of hunger.

Most fat digestion happens after fat passes from the stomach to the small intestine. Once the fatty residue moves inside the small intestine, the smallest fatty acids and glycerol are able to pass through the intestinal wall into the blood. They are transported to the liver where they are converted into energy and other fats as needed. Sometimes the liver stores fat, which is not a healthy condition.

The larger triglycerides are broken down in the small intestine by bile, an emulsifier that is made in the liver and stored in the gallbladder. Bile emulsifies fats by breaking them down with watery digestive secretions and prepares them for additional breakdown by enzymes. The pancreas then secretes a digestive enzyme into the small intestine, which breaks down the emulsified triglycerides even further.

FAT ABSORPTION

Fatty acids and cholesterol cannot easily travel in the blood or in the lymph, a watery body fluid that carries the products of fat digestion. This is because they are large molecules, and fat and water do not mix (think oil and vinegar salad dressing that must be shaken before using).

To compensate, fatty acids are packaged inside a protein "shell" for their journey through the bloodstream. These protein packages are called lipoproteins, which means lipids (fats) and protein. The two most well known types of lipoproteins are low-density lipoproteins (LDL) and high-density lipoproteins (HDL), both discussed in regards to cholesterol on page 9.

HDLs contain the most protein and the least fats and carry cholesterol to the liver for recycling or disposal, while LDLs contain mostly cholesterol. This protein to fat ratio is another reason why HDLs are considered to be "good" cholesterol and LDLs "bad" cholesterol for the body.

The fatty acids that are not used by the body are returned to the liver for recycling, disposal or storage. Excess fat in the diet may contribute to greater fat stores. But on a ketogenic diet fat is converted into energy. The majority of body cells can use fatty acids for energy when glucose is not available, except for those in the brain, eyes and red blood cells that rely upon glucose.

When carbohydrates are limited, as in the ketogenic diet, the brain can still obtain a small amount of glucose from a process called gluconeogenesis (glucose production from fats and proteins). On a ketogenic diet, the brain mainly uses ketones for one-half to three-quarters of its energy needs. This process was likely created as a survival mechanism by the body when carbohydrates were limited.

FAT METABOLISM

After dietary fats are digested and absorbed they can be channeled into energy production. Additionally, enzymes can break down stored fats to release fatty acids into the bloodstream. When these fatty acids reach the muscle cells, they go into the powerhouse of the cell, called the mitochondria.

In the mitochondria, energy (calories) is removed from the fatty acids that produce chemical energy for metabolism. Carbon dioxide and water are by-products.

Fats supply about twice the amount of calories for chemical energy production than carbohydrates or protein: 9 calories per gram for fats compared to 4 calories per gram for both carbohydrates and protein. This is why fats and oils are so calorie (and energy) dense.

Another method of fat metabolism or breakdown for energy is called ketosis. Ketosis occurs when there are little to no carbohydrates (the body's preferred energy source) in the diet.

Ketosis may occur in prolonged starvation or during higher-protein diets that greatly reduce carbohydrate intake. Ketosis utilizes ketones, the by-products of stored fats, rather than carbohydrates (namely glucose) for energy.

FAT STORAGE

Fats that are not used by the body are generally stored in fat cells. Fat cells store small amounts of fat molecules when the concentration of fatty acids in the blood rises, such as after a high-fat meal or snack. An increase in fatty acids in the blood triggers an enzyme called lipase (located in fat tissue) to convert the fatty acids from the blood into a storage form within the fat cells.

The majority of stored fat in the human body is under the skin, called subcutaneous fat. A high percentage of subcutaneous fat surrounds the buttocks, breasts, hips and waist in females—likely for reproduction purposes. In males, most subcutaneous fat is found around the abdomen, buttocks and chest. There is also fat around the kidneys, liver and inside muscles. A goal in a well-designed diet program is to reduce extraneous fat—especially the fat that surrounds the organs and muscles.

METABOLISM: FATS VERSUS CARBOHYDRATES

Since the 1950's, Americans were advised to reduce fat in their diet for heart disease protection, weight loss and weight maintenance and well-being. Dietary approaches were low in fat and cholesterol and higher in carbohydrates (starches and sugars), while higher protein and fat diets were criticized for promoting rich foods and beverages and contributing to elevated blood cholesterol.

During the 1990's when high carbohydrate diets were at their peak in popularity, obesity rates began to rise. Total calories were implicated in these increases, but also the amounts of carbohydrates in the American diet—particularly processed carbohydrates from refined breadstuffs and sugar-filled beverages—were linked with the rise in obesity.

Subsequently, new research demonstrated that low-carbohydrate, higher-fat diets actually improve HDL-cholesterol and do not significantly increase LDL-cholesterol. An examination of carbohydrate metabolism versus fat metabolism explains how this can be possible.

Your body must maintain its blood sugar within a certain range for sufficient energy to think, work, exercise and perform other activities. Insulin, a hormone produced by the pancreas, helps to shift blood sugar (glucose) into the cells for these functions.

Dietary carbohydrates in the form of starches and sugars supply your body with these needed carbohydrates. The body also has a limited store of glycogen or stored carbohydrates—about 2,500 calories—in reserve that are contained within the blood, liver and muscles. However, this amount can quickly be expended to meet the increased energy demands during disease states, exercise and fasting.

In contrast, your body has about 50,000 calories of stored fat with potential energy that can be converted into energy through a complex series of chemical reactions.

After eating or drinking, insulin moves blood sugar (glucose) into the cells for energy; blood sugar returns to normal levels and you get hungry, eat, and the process repeats. If the pancreas does not produce enough insulin (as in diabetes), this may damage the small blood vessels in the body and blindness, heart attack, infections, kidney disease, stroke or poor wound healing may result. Either oral or injected insulin may be needed—also as in diabetes.

If the body runs out of stored carbohydrates, then the liver produces ketones that can be converted into energy in ketosis (described in Fat Metabolism on page 15). A higher-fat lower-carb diet encourages the body to use ketosis for energy production, sparing glucose for the brain, eyes and red blood cells. This shift in energy metabolism generally results in weight loss. Depending upon the degree of ketosis, weight loss may be significant. An in-depth discussion about the ketogenic diet and dieting follows this section.

Carbohydrates contain water, so part of the initial weight loss in a higher protein and fat and lower carbohydrate diet is the decrease in water stores. This is partially the reason why the initial weight loss at the beginning of a ketogenic diet may be significant. Another reason may be that a ketogenic diet differs significantly in food and beverage choices from a standard diet.

There may be some temporary side effects on a ketogenic diet, such as fatigue, light-headedness and/or increased urination. It is important to check first with a healthcare provider before beginning a ketogenic diet—or any diet.

Refined carbohydrates (especially those low in fat) are processed very quickly, and may first spike and then plunge blood sugar levels. Low-fat, refined carbohydrate-containing foods are also quite unsatisfying, which may backfire and cause a person to overeat. Initially the decrease in carbohydrates may be physically and emotionally discomforting, but once the body adjusts to a ketogenic state, more protein and fat in the diet may be satiating. Since fat has twice as many calories per gram as carbohydrates, you may find that you'll actually be more satisfied with less food.

Beef and Pepper Kabobs
(page 60)

Mesquite-Grilled Salmon Fillets
(page 120)

THE KETOGENIC DIET AND DIETING

The ketogenic diet is hardly new. The idea that fasting could be used as a therapy to treat disease was one that ancient Greek and Indian physicians embraced. "On the Sacred Disease", an early treatise in the Hippocratic Corpus, proposed how dietary modifications could be useful in epileptic management. Hippocrates, a Greek physician called the Father of Modern Medicine, wrote in "Epidemics" how abstinence from food and drink cured epilepsy.

In the 20th century, the first ketogenic diet became popularized in the 1920's and 1930's as a regimen for treating epilepsy and an alternative to non-mainstream fasting. It was also promoted as a means of restoring health. In 1921, the ketogenic diet was officially established when an endocrinologist noted that three water-soluble compounds were produced by the liver as a result of following a diet that was rich in fat and low in carbohydrates. The term "water diet" had been used prior to this time to describe a diet that was free of starch and sugar. This is because when carbohydrates are broken down by the body carbon dioxide and water are by-products. When newer, anticonvulsant therapies were established, the ketogenic diet was temporarily abandoned.

In the 1960's the ketogenic diet was revisited when it was noted that more ketones are produced by medium chain triglycerides (MCTs) per unit of energy than by normal dietary fats (mostly long-chain triglycerides) because MCTs are quickly transported to the liver to be metabolized. In research diets where about 60 percent of the calories came from MCT oil, more protein and up to about three times as many carbohydrates could be consumed in comparison to "classic" ketogenic diets. This is why MCT oil is included in some ketogenic diets today.

In the 1950's and 1960's many versions of the ketogenic diet were popularized as high-protein, low-carbohydrate and a quick method of weight loss. Also at this time, the risk factors of excess fat and protein in the diet were criticized for being detrimental to health. Outside of the medical community, the ketogenic diet was not widely recognized for its therapeutic benefits so response to it was sensational in scope.

Then in the 1980's the Glycemic Index (GI) of foods and beverages was revealed that accounted for the differences in the speed of digestion of different types of carbohydrates. This explanation became the springboard for a number of ketogenic diets that were revised from years earlier. By the late 1990's the low-carb craze became one of the most popular types of dieting. Since this time, the original ketogenic diet underwent many refinements and hybrid diets developed.

Variations of the ketogenic diet continued to surface throughout the 20th century since the premise of the ketogenic diet—higher fat and protein and low carbohydrate—was used to treat diabetes and induce weight loss among other applications.

Table 1 summarizes the basics of the ketogenic diet. Many clinical studies examined its effectiveness and safety, and advantages and drawbacks were identified (see **Table 2**).

TABLE 1

KETOGENIC DIET BASICS

Generally, the percentages of macronutrients on a ketogenic diet are as follows:
- **Fat** 60 to 75 percent of total daily calories
- **Protein** 15 to 30 percent of total daily calories
- **Carbohydrates** 5 to 10 percent of total daily calories

Both fat and protein have high priority on a ketogenic diet, with non-starchy carbohydrates completing the remaining calories. While calories are not as important on the ketogenic diet as they are for other diets, a closer examination of the contributions of these macronutrients helps to put the amounts into perspective.

If total daily calories were about 2,000, then the percentages of macronutrients on a ketogenic diet would resemble the following amounts:
- **Fat** 60 to 75 percent of total daily calories or about 1,200 to 1,500 calories
- **Protein** 15 to 30 percent of total daily calories or about 300 to 600 calories
- **Carbohydrates** 5 to 10 percent of total daily calories or about 100 to 200 calories

In selecting foods and beverages, think protein and fat first, then non-starchy carbohydrates to complete. Until you truly have a handle on what constitutes low carbohydrates, find a carbohydrate counter to help to keep you in line. The ketogenic diet meal suggestions in **Table 5** (page 25) may help your food and beverage selections.

TABLE 2

ADVANTAGES AND DRAWBACKS OF KETOGENIC DIETS

ADVANTAGES
- No calorie counting or focus on portion sizes
- Initial weight loss
- After initial transition, hunger subsides
- Improved energy
- Improved blood pressure
- Improved blood fats: high-density lipoproteins, cholesterol, low-density lipoproteins, triglycerides
- Reduced blood sugar, C-reactive protein (marker of inflammation), insulin, waist circumference
- Significant short-term weight loss possible

DRAWBACKS
- Hard to sustain
- Limited food choices
- May lead to taste fatigue
- Socialization difficult
- Digestive issues (such as constipation, fatty stool, nausea)
- Nutrient deficiencies (such as calcium, vitamins A, C, D, B-vitamins, fiber, magnesium, selenium)
- Fiber, vitamin and mineral supplements suggested
- Increased urination (bladder, kidney contraindications)
- Diabetes issues
- Rapid, sizeable short-term weight loss concerning; long-term weight maintenance questionable

FAT IN HEALTH AND DISEASE

Fats are essential to the diet and health for many purposes. Fats function as the body's thermostat. The layer of fat just beneath the skin helps to keep the body warm or causes it to perspire to cool the body.

Fat contributes to bile acids, cell membranes and steroid hormones (such as estrogen and testosterone), cushions the body from shock and helps to regulate fluid balance. Too many or too few fats in the diet may influence each of these important body functions.

One of the most important roles of fat in the body is as an energy source, especially when carbohydrates are not available from the diet or are lacking in the body. When people did manual work all day and expended the calories that they consumed, they made good use of carbohydrates and fats in their diet and within their energy stores. Today's laborsaving devices and sedentary lifestyles create less need for excess carbohydrate calories— particularly if they are refined. Even a plant-based diet may be unnecessarily high in refined carbohydrate calories.

Over the years, as humans moved from a plant-based diet toward an animal-based diet, the composition of fatty acids in the American diet switched from monounsaturated and polyunsaturated fats to more saturated fats, which are associated more with cardiovascular disease. A diet that is only filled with saturated fats may not be healthy. By incorporating avocado, fish, nuts, oils and seeds and other foods that contain monounsaturated and polyunsaturated fats into your diet this may help to support a healthier proportion of fats in the body for weight maintenance and good health.

Besides cardiovascular disease, excess saturated and trans fats in the human diet are associated with certain cancers, cerebral vascular disease, diabetes, obesity and metabolic syndrome, which is a collection of conditions that may include abnormal cholesterol or triglyceride levels, excess body fat around the waist, high blood sugar and increased blood pressure that may increase a person's risk of diabetes, heart disease and/or stroke.

THE CHOLESTEROL CONTROVERSY

Atherosclerosis, or hardening of the arteries, is not a modern disease. Rather, the association between blood cholesterol and cardiovascular disease was recognized as far back as the 1850's.

One hundred years later in the 1950's, cholesterol and saturated fats in the diet were implicated as major risk factors for cardiovascular disease. Then in the 1980's, major US health institutions established that the process of lowering blood cholesterol (specifically LDL-cholesterol) reduces the risk of heart attacks that are caused by coronary heart disease.

Some scientists questioned this conclusion that marked the unofficial start of what's been called the "cholesterol controversy". Studies of cholesterol-lowering drugs known as statins supported the idea that reducing blood cholesterol means less mortality from heart disease.

Subsequent statin studies have questioned this association. Other factors aside from dietary cholesterol have since been identified that may lead to elevated blood cholesterol, such as trans fats.

The liver manufactures cholesterol, so reducing cholesterol in the diet should help to reduce blood cholesterol, coronary heart disease and the risk of heart attack. But in some individuals, the liver produces more cholesterol than the body requires and cardiovascular disease may still develop. Accordingly, dietary cholesterol does not necessarily predict cardiovascular disease or a heart attack.

While dietary cholesterol may be a measure for greater cardiovascular risks, cardiovascular disease and heart attacks are also dependent upon such lifestyle and genetic factors as age, diet, exercise, gender, genetics, medication and stress. Reducing hydrogenated fats, saturated fats and trans fats; incorporating mono- and polyunsaturated fats and losing weight to help better manage blood fats are other sensible measures to take.

Longer-term weight management is also a preventative measure in cardiovascular disease. Reducing cholesterol and saturated fat in the diet while integrating foods and beverages with mono- and polyunsaturated fats and oils, dietary fiber, antioxidants and other phytonutrients may lead to a decrease in overall calorie consumption and weight loss and an improvement in overall health.

Stuffed Mushroom Caps
(page 174)

SO WHAT (AND HOW) SHOULD I EAT?

If you want to lose body fat, then the general consensus is that you need to take in fewer calories than you burn for energy. For example, if you're an average woman over 40, decreasing your caloric intake may be a reasonable starting point. If you are of shorter stature and/or very inactive, or you haven't dropped any pounds after a few weeks, you may consider lowering your daily intake of calories by 100-calorie increments until you start seeing weight loss. But don't go much below 1,000 calories without your health care provider's supervision. (And be sure to check with your health care provider before making any major changes to your diet or activity level, especially if you have any serious health problems.)

The ketogenic diet is another approach to weight loss, one that does not focus on calories. Instead, it focuses on the composition of calories from fats, proteins and carbohydrates.

Fats are satisfying because they take longer for the body to digest, and some are converted into ketones for energy. You don't want to skimp on proteins because protein helps maintain and build calorie-burning muscle and also keeps you satiated between meals. Choose protein sources that supply monounsaturated fats and other heart-healthy unsaturated fats; good options include fish, seafood, nuts and seeds. (Fatty fish, such as herring, mackerel, salmon and tuna contain polyunsaturated fats—especially disease-fighting omega-3 fatty acids). You'll need to replace highly processed and refined foods that are full of saturated and trans fats, sugar and refined carbohydrates with minimally processed fiber- and nutrient-rich foods that include non-starchy vegetables.

What you'll likely end up with is a satisfying eating plan with ample protein, healthy fats and minimal carbohydrates that may help you to feel full and lose weight in the process. It's also a plan that may help you to maintain weight loss over time in a modified manner.

If you've ever tried to lose weight before, you know how quickly between-meal hunger may sabotage your best efforts. When your stomach starts rumbling hours before your next meal, it's tempting to grab whatever is available. Often, that "whatever" is some unhealthy packaged snack food or beverage that is loaded with empty calories, sodium, sugars and/or unhealthy fats. Or, if you manage to ignore this hunger, you may become so ravenous at the next meal that you consume far more calories than your body actually needs.

To prevent hunger from spoiling your weight-loss efforts, eat when you are hungry and stop eating when you are full, whether a meal or snack. Try to consume meals and snacks that include a source of hunger-fighting protein and healthy fat, and count your carbs so as not to exceed the daily limit of 20 to 50 grams of non-starchy carbohydrates.

Drink plenty of water throughout the day (especially if you live in a hot climate or sweat excessively) since ketogenic diets tend to be dehydrating and may lead to fatigue or ill feelings. This may be due to an imbalance of electrolytes; specifically sodium that the kidneys excrete during ketosis. Sometimes lightly salting your food may help to restore sodium. A high-quality vitamin and mineral supplement is also sensible.

TABLE 3

ACCEPTABLE FOODS, BEVERAGES AND INGREDIENTS FOR KETOGENIC DIETS

BEVERAGES
- Broth
- Hard liquor
- Nut milks
- Unsweetened coffee, tea
- Water

EGGS
- Egg whites
- Powdered eggs
- Whole eggs

FATS AND OILS
- Butter
- Cocoa butter
- Coconut butter, cream and oil
- Ghee
- Lard
- Oils: avocado oil, macadamia nut oil, MCT oil, olive oil and cold-pressed vegetable oils (flax, safflower, soybean)
- Mayonnaise

FISH AND SEAFOOD
- Anchovies
- Fish (catfish, cod, flounder, halibut, mackerel, mahi-mahi, salmon, snapper, trout, tuna)
- Shellfish (clams, crab, lobster, mussels, oysters, scallops, squid)

FRUITS AND VEGETABLES
- Avocados
- Cruciferous vegetables (broccoli, Brussels sprouts, cabbage, cauliflower, kohlrabi)
- Fermented vegetables (kimchi, sauerkraut)
- Leafy greens (bok choy, chard, endive, lettuce, kale, radicchio, spinach, watercress)
- Lemon and lime juice and zest
- Mushrooms
- Non-starchy vegetables (asparagus, bamboo shoots, celery, cucumber)
- Seaweed and kelp
- Squash (spaghetti squash, yellow squash, zucchini)
- Tomatoes used in moderation in some keto diets)

DAIRY PRODUCTS
- Crème fraîche
- Greek yogurt
- Hard cheese (aged Cheddar, feta, Parmesan, Swiss)
- Heavy cream
- Soft cheese (Brie, blue, Colby, Monterey Jack, mozzarella)
- Sour cream
- Spreadable cheese (cream cheese, cottage cheese and mascarpone)

MEATS AND POULTRY
- Beef (ground beef, roasts, steak, stew meat)
- Goat (leg, loin, rack, saddle, shoulder)
- Lamb (leg, loin, rack, ribs, shank, shoulder)
- Organ meats (heart, kidneys, liver, tongue)
- Poultry with skin (such as chicken, duck, pheasant, quail, turkey)
- Pork (bacon and sausage without fillers, ground pork, ham, pork chops, pork loin, tenderloin)
- Tofu used in moderation in some keto diets)
- Veal (double, flank, leg, rib, shoulder, sirloin)

NON-DAIRY BEVERAGES
- Almond milk
- Cashew milk
- Coconut milk
- Soymilk (used in moderation in some keto diets)

NUTS AND SEEDS
- Nut butters (almond, macadamia)
- Seeds (chia, flax, poppy, sesame, sunflower)
- Whole nuts (almonds, Brazil nuts, macadamia, pecans, hazelnuts, peanuts, pine nuts, walnuts)

PANTRY ITEMS
- Herbs (dried or fresh such as basil, cilantro, oregano, parsley, rosemary and thyme)
- Horseradish
- Hot sauce
- Mustard
- Pepper
- Pesto sauce
- Pickles
- Salad dressings (without sweeteners)
- Salt
- Spices (such as ground red pepper, chili powder, cinnamon and cumin)
- Unsweetened gelatin
- Vinegar
- Whey protein (unsweetened)
- Worcestershire sauce

TABLE 4

UNACCEPTABLE FOODS, BEVERAGES AND INGREDIENTS FOR KETOGENIC DIETS

- Alcohol other than hard liquor (beer, sugary alcoholic beverages, wine)
- Beans
- Breads and breadstuffs
- Cakes and pastries
- Candy
- Cereals
- Cookies
- Crackers
- Flours
- Fruit, all (fresh, dried)
- Grains (amaranth, barley, buckwheat, bulgur, corn, millet, oats, rice, rye, sorghum, sprouted grains, wheat)
- Legumes (lentils, peas)
- Margarines with trans fats
- Milk (some full-fat milk is acceptable in some ketogenic diets)
- Oats and muesli
- Potatoes, all kinds (white, yellow, sweet)
- Quinoa
- Pasta
- Pizza
- Processed and refined snack foods
- Rice
- Root vegetables
- Soda
- Sports drinks
- Sugar and honey
- Syrup
- Wheat gluten
- Yams

NOTES ON KETOGENIC FOODS, BEVERAGES AND INGREDIENTS

In general, the foods, beverages and ingredients that are included in a ketogenic diet incorporate eggs, healthy fats and oils, fish, meats and organ meats and non-starchy vegetables. These "acceptable" foods, beverages and ingredients contain protein and fats and are low in carbohydrates that contribute to the effectiveness of ketogenic diets. They are listed in **Table 3 – Acceptable Foods, Beverages and Ingredients for Ketogenic Diets**.

In **Table 4 – Unacceptable Foods, Beverages and Ingredients for Ketogenic Diets** are shown. While there is a wide-range of ketogenic diet approaches, these foods, beverages and ingredients are generally considered to be "unacceptable" on many ketogenic diets. In general, their carbohydrate content exceeds what is considered as optimal for effective ketosis and diet success.

TABLE 5
SAMPLE KETOGENIC DIET MEALS:
BREAKFAST, LUNCH, DINNER AND SNACKS

Examples of combinations of protein + low-carb, non-starchy vegetables + fats:

BREAKFAST:

- Almond, coconut, hemp or other nut or seed milks or beverages (unsweetened)
- Bacon, sausage or sliced meats (without carbohydrate fillers)
- Cheese, hard or soft varieties
- Eggs, scrambled or fried + vegetables (asparagus, broccoli, garlic, mushrooms, onions or spinach) + coconut or olive oil + avocado, olives, salsa and/or sour cream
- Greek yogurt with nut butter, chia or flax seeds, herbs and spices (cinnamon, ginger or nutmeg)
- Smoked fish (such as lox, sable or whitefish)
- Smoothies made with keto-friendly ingredients (protein powder, almond or coconut butter, avocado, cocoa powder, chia or flax seeds, spices such as cinnamon, smoked paprika or turmeric and unsweetened almond or hemp milk)
- Vegetable slices (cucumber or zucchini or lettuce) topped with cheese

LUNCH AND DINNER:

- Eggs + watercress or spinach + avocado dressing
- Lamb + kale + sesame oil
- Pork + cauliflower + coconut butter
- Poultry + zucchini and yellow squash + extra virgin olive oil
- Salmon + broccoli + mustard sauce
- Sardines + cucumbers and onions + sour cream dressing
- Seafood + leafy green salad + oil and vinegar dressing
- Steak + asparagus + butter sauce
- Tofu + mushrooms and bok choy + ghee
- Tuna + celery + mayonnaise

SNACKS:

- Asparagus with goat cheese dip
- Avocado filled hard-cooked eggs
- Celery + nut or seed butter
- Cheese + olive skewers
- Chia and flaxseed crackers + cream cheese
- Cucumber and cream cheese spread
- Cream cheese and bacon stuffed celery
- Deviled eggs with fresh herbs and chives
- Greek yogurt with chopped cucumbers and garlic
- Guacamole with onions and garlic
- Ham and cheddar or Swiss cheese roll ups
- Mixed nut-coated cheese balls
- Nut butters (such as almond) blended with ricotta cheese
- Olives stuffed with blue cheese
- Parmesan cheese crisps
- Seeds and seed butters such as tahini
- Sliced jicama with herbed cream cheese

BREAKFAST

CALIFORNIA OMELET WITH AVOCADO

MAKES 4 SERVINGS

1. Combine tomatoes, cilantro and ¼ teaspoon salt in small bowl; set aside.

2. Whisk eggs and milk in medium bowl until well blended; season with salt and pepper.

3. Heat small nonstick skillet over medium heat; spray with nonstick cooking spray. Pour half of egg mixture into skillet; cook 2 minutes or until eggs begin to set. Lift edge of omelet to allow uncooked portion to flow underneath. Cook 3 minutes or until set.

4. Spoon half of tomato mixture over half of omelet. Loosen omelet with spatula and fold in half. Slide omelet onto serving plates. Repeat steps for second omelet. Serve topped with avocado and cucumber; garnish with lemon wedges.

6 ounces plum tomato, chopped (about 1½ tomatoes)

2 to 4 tablespoons chopped fresh cilantro

¼ teaspoon salt

8 eggs

¼ cup milk

Salt and black pepper

1 ripe medium avocado, diced

1 small cucumber, chopped

1 lemon, quartered (optional)

Calories 145, Total Fat 5g, Carbs 13g, Net Carbs 9g, Fiber 4g, Protein 14g

SPICY CRABMEAT FRITTATA

MAKES 4 SERVINGS

1. Preheat broiler. Pick out and discard any shell or cartilage from crabmeat; break up large pieces of crabmeat.

2. Beat eggs in medium bowl. Add crabmeat, salt, black pepper and hot pepper sauce; mix well.

3. Heat oil in large ovenproof skillet over medium-high heat. Add bell pepper and garlic; cook and stir 3 minutes or until tender. Add tomato; cook and stir 1 minute. Reduce heat to medium-low. Stir in egg mixture; cook 7 minutes or until eggs begin to set around edges.

4. Transfer skillet to broiler. Broil 4 inches from heat source 1 to 2 minutes or until frittata is golden brown and center is set.

1 can (about 6 ounces) lump white crabmeat, drained

6 eggs

¼ teaspoon salt

¼ teaspoon black pepper

¼ teaspoon hot pepper sauce

1 tablespoon olive oil

1 green bell pepper, finely chopped

2 cloves garlic, minced

1 plum tomato, seeded and finely chopped

Calories 187, Total Fat 11g, Carbs 4g, Net Carbs 3g, Fiber 1g, Protein 17g

GREEK ISLES OMELET

MAKES 2 SERVINGS

1. Spray small nonstick skillet with nonstick cooking spray; heat over medium heat. Add onion; cook and stir 2 minutes or until crisp-tender. Add artichokes; cook and stir until heated through. Add spinach, tomato and olives; gently stir. Remove to small bowl.

2. Wipe out skillet with paper towels and spray with cooking spray. Whisk eggs in medium bowl until well blended; season with salt and pepper. Heat skillet over medium heat. Pour egg mixture into skillet; cook and stir gently, lifting edge to allow uncooked portion to flow underneath. Continue cooking until set.

3. Spoon vegetable mixture over half of omelet; gently loosen omelet with spatula and fold in half. Cut in half; serve immediately.

¼ cup chopped onion

¼ cup canned artichoke hearts, rinsed and drained

¼ cup chopped spinach

¼ cup chopped plum tomato

2 tablespoons sliced pitted black olives, rinsed and drained

4 eggs

Salt and black pepper

Calories 111, Total Fat 3g, Carbs 7g, Net Carbs 6g, Fiber 1g, Protein 13g

CHEDDARY SAUSAGE FRITTATA

MAKES 4 SERVINGS

1. Preheat broiler. Whisk eggs and milk in medium bowl until well blended.

2. Heat 12-inch ovenproof nonstick skillet over medium-high heat. Add sausage; cook and stir 4 minutes or until no longer pink, stirring to break up meat. Transfer sausage to paper towels with slotted spoon. Drain fat.

3. Add pepper to same skillet; cook and stir 2 minutes or until crisp-tender. Return sausage to skillet. Add egg mixture; stir until blended. Cover; cook over medium-low heat 10 minutes or until eggs are almost set.

4. Sprinkle cheese over frittata; broil 2 minutes or until cheese is melted. Cut into 4 wedges. Serve immediately.

TIP: If skillet is not ovenproof, wrap handle in heavy-duty foil.

4 eggs

¼ cup milk

1 package (12 ounces) bulk pork breakfast sausage

1 poblano pepper, seeded and chopped

1 cup (4 ounces) shredded Cheddar cheese

Calories 423, Total Fat 31g, Carbs 4g, Net Carbs 3g, Fiber 1g, Protein 27g

ZUCCHINI-TOMATO FRITTATA

MAKES 4 SERVINGS

1. Preheat broiler. Whisk whole eggs, egg whites, cottage cheese, tomatoes, green onions, basil and ground red pepper in medium bowl; mix well. Season with salt and black pepper.

2. Spray 10-inch ovenproof skillet with nonstick cooking spray; heat over medium-high heat. Add zucchini, broccoli and bell pepper; cook and stir 3 to 4 minutes or until crisp-tender.

3. Pour egg mixture over vegetables in skillet. Cook, uncovered, gently lifting sides of frittata so uncooked egg flows underneath. Cook 7 to 8 minutes or until frittata is almost firm and golden brown on bottom. Remove from heat. Sprinkle with Parmesan.

4. Broil about 5 inches from heat 3 to 5 minutes or until golden brown on surface. Garnish with paprika, if desired. Cut into 4 wedges. Serve immediately.

3 whole eggs

5 egg whites

$1/2$ cup cottage cheese

$1/2$ cup rehydrated* sun-dried tomatoes (1 ounce dry), coarsely chopped

$1/4$ cup chopped green onions

$1/4$ cup chopped fresh basil

$1/8$ teaspoon ground red pepper

   Salt and black pepper

1 cup sliced zucchini

1 cup broccoli florets

1 cup diced red or yellow bell pepper

2 tablespoons grated Parmesan cheese

   Paprika (optional)

*To rehydrate sun-dried tomatoes, pour 1 cup boiling water over tomatoes in small bowl. Let soak 5 to 10 minutes or until softened; drain well.

Calories 160, Total Fat 5g, Carbs 13g, Net Carbs 10g, Fiber 3g, Protein 16g

CRUSTLESS SOUTHWESTERN QUICHE

MAKES 4 SERVINGS

1. Preheat oven to 400°F. Grease 10-inch quiche dish or deep-dish pie plate.

2. Remove sausage from casings. Crumble sausage into medium skillet. Cook over medium heat until sausage is browned, stirring to break up meat. Remove from heat; pour off drippings. Cool 5 minutes.

3. Whisk eggs in medium bowl. Stir in spinach, cheese, cream and sausage; mix well. Pour into prepared quiche dish. Bake 20 minutes or until center is set. Let stand 5 minutes. Cut into 4 wedges. Serve with salsa.

8 ounces chorizo sausage*

8 eggs

1 package (10 ounces) frozen chopped spinach, thawed and squeezed dry

1 cup crumbled queso fresco or shredded Cheddar or pepper Jack cheese

1/2 cup whipping cream or half-and-half

1/4 cup salsa

Chorizo, a spicy Mexican pork sausage, is flavored with garlic and chiles. It is available in most supermarkets. If it is not available, substitute 8 ounces bulk pork sausage plus 1/4 teaspoon ground red pepper.

Calories 583, Total Fat 45g, Carbs 9g, Net Carbs 7g, Fiber 2g, Protein 36g

SPICY SCRAMBLED EGGS WITH TOMATOES AND PEPPERS

MAKES 4 SERVINGS

1. Whisk eggs and salt in medium bowl.

2. Heat butter and oil in large skillet over medium heat until hot. Add onion and peppers; cook and stir 45 seconds or until hot but not soft.

3. Stir in tomatoes. Increase heat to medium-high; cook and stir 45 seconds or until tomatoes are hot.

4. Add egg mixture to skillet. Cook without stirring 1 minute. Cook 2 to 3 minutes more, stirring lightly until eggs are softly set.

NOTE: Fresh chiles provide crunchy texture that cannot be duplicated with canned chiles. For milder flavor, remove the seeds from some or all of the chiles.

8 eggs

$\frac{1}{2}$ teaspoon salt

2 tablespoons butter

2 tablespoons vegetable oil

$\frac{1}{3}$ cup finely chopped onion

2 to 4 fresh serrano peppers, finely chopped

2 medium tomatoes, seeded, chopped and drained

Calories 282, Total Fat 23g, Carbs 5g, Net Carbs 4g, Fiber 1g, Protein 13g

KETO BREAD

MAKES 16 SLICES

1. Preheat oven to 375°F. Generously grease 8×4-inch loaf pan with 1 tablespoon butter. Melt remaining 6 tablespoons butter; cool slightly.

2. Combine almond flour, baking powder and salt in medium bowl. Add melted butter and 5 egg yolks stir until blended.

3. Place egg whites and cream of tartar in bowl of stand mixer; attach whip attachment to mixer. Whip egg whites on high speed 1 to 2 minutes or until stiff peaks form.

4. Stir one third of egg whites into almond flour mixture until well blended. Gently fold in remaining egg whites until thoroughly blended. Scrape batter into prepared pan; smooth top.

5. Bake 25 to 30 minutes or until top is light brown and dry and toothpick inserted into center comes out clean. Cool in pan on wire rack 10 minutes. Remove from pan; cool completely.

- 7 tablespoons butter, divided
- 2 cups almond flour
- 3$\frac{1}{2}$ teaspoons baking powder
- $\frac{1}{2}$ teaspoon salt
- 6 eggs at room temperature, separated*
- $\frac{1}{4}$ teaspoon cream of tartar

Discard 1 egg yolk.

Calories 156, Total Fat 13g, Carbs 4g, Net Carbs 2g, Fiber 2g, Protein 5g

MEAT

SAUSAGE AND PEPPERS

MAKES 4 SERVINGS

1. Fill medium saucepan half full with water; bring to a boil over high heat. Add sausage; cook 5 minutes over medium heat. Drain and cut diagonally into 1-inch slices.

2. Heat oil in large (12-inch) cast iron skillet over medium-high heat. Add sausage; cook about 10 minutes or until browned, stirring occasionally. Remove sausage to plate; set aside.

3. Add onions, bell peppers, 1 teaspoon salt and oregano to skillet; cook over medium heat about 25 minutes or until vegetables are very soft and browned in spots, stirring occasionally.

4. Stir sausage and remaining $1/2$ teaspoon salt into skillet; cook 3 minutes or until heated through.

1 pound uncooked hot or mild Italian sausage links

2 tablespoons olive oil

3 medium onions, cut into $1/2$-inch slices

2 red bell peppers, cut into $1/2$-inch slices

2 green bell peppers, cut into $1/2$-inch slices

$1^{1}/_{2}$ teaspoons coarse salt, divided

1 teaspoon dried oregano

Calories 510, Total Fat 43g, Carbs 15g, Net Carbs 11g, Fiber 4g, Protein 18g

FRENCH QUARTER STEAKS

MAKES 2 SERVINGS

1. Combine water, Worcestershire sauce, soy sauce, chili powder, 2 cloves garlic, paprika, red pepper, 1 teaspoon black pepper and onion powder in small bowl; mix well. Place steaks in large resealable food storage bag; pour marinade over steaks. Seal bag; turn to coat. Marinate in refrigerator 1 to 3 hours.

2. Remove steaks from marinade 30 minutes before cooking; discard marinade and pat steaks dry with paper towel. Oil grid. Prepare grill for direct cooking.

3. While grill is preheating, heat 1 tablespoon butter and oil in large skillet over medium high heat. Add onion; cook 5 minutes, stirring occasionally. Add mushrooms, $1/4$ teaspoon salt and remaining $1/4$ teaspoon black pepper; cook 10 minutes or until onion is golden brown and mushrooms are beginning to brown, stirring occasionally. Combine remaining 2 tablespoons butter, 1 clove garlic and $1/8$ teaspoon salt in small skillet; cook over medium-low heat 3 minutes or until garlic begins to sizzle.

4. Grill steaks over medium-high heat 6 minutes; turn and grill 6 minutes for medium rare or until desired doneness. Brush both sides of steaks with garlic butter during last 2 minutes of cooking. Remove to plate and tent with foil; let rest 5 minutes. Serve steaks with onion and mushroom mixture.

$1/2$ cup water

2 tablespoons Worcestershire sauce

2 tablespoons soy sauce

1 tablespoon chili powder

3 cloves garlic, minced, divided

2 teaspoons paprika

$1\frac{1}{2}$ teaspoons ground red pepper

$1\frac{1}{4}$ teaspoons black pepper, divided

1 teaspoon onion powder

2 top sirloin steaks (about 8 ounces each), 1 inch thick)

3 tablespoons butter, divided

1 tablespoon olive oil

$1/2$ large onion, thinly sliced

8 ounces sliced mushrooms (white, cremini and/or shiitake)

$1/4$ teaspoon plus $1/8$ teaspoon salt, divided

Calories 520, Total Fat 33g, Carbs 9g, Net Carbs 7g, Fiber 2g, Protein 47g

GREEK-STYLE BEEF KABOBS

MAKES 4 SERVINGS

1. Combine beef, salad dressing, 2 tablespoons lemon juice, oregano, Worcestershire sauce, basil, lemon peel, 1 teaspoon salt and red pepper flakes in large resealable food storage bag. Seal bag; turn to coat. Marinate in refrigerator at least 8 hours or overnight, turning occasionally.

2. Preheat broiler. Remove beef from marinade; reserve marinade. Thread beef, bell pepper and tomatoes alternately onto 4 (10-inch) skewers.* Spray rimmed baking sheet or broiler pan with nonstick cooking spray. Brush kabobs with marinade; place on baking sheet. Discard remaining marinade. Broil kabobs 3 minutes. Turn over; broil 2 minutes or until desired doneness is reached. *Do not overcook.* Remove skewers to serving platter.

3. Add remaining 1 tablespoon lemon juice, oil and remaining $\frac{1}{8}$ teaspoon salt to pan drippings on baking sheet; stir well, scraping bottom of pan with flat spatula. Pour juices over kabobs.

If using wooden skewers, soak in water 25 to 30 minutes before using to prevent burning.

- 1 pound beef top sirloin steak (1 inch thick), cut into 16 pieces
- ¼ cup fat-free Italian salad dressing
- 3 tablespoons fresh lemon juice, divided
- 1 tablespoon dried oregano
- 1 tablespoon Worcestershire sauce
- 2 teaspoons dried basil
- 1 teaspoon grated lemon peel
- 1⅛ teaspoons salt, divided
- ⅛ teaspoon red pepper flakes
- 1 large green bell pepper, cut into 16 pieces
- 16 cherry tomatoes
- 2 teaspoons olive oil

Calories 193, Total Fat 8g, Carbs 5g, Net Carbs 4g, Fiber 1g, Protein 25g

PORK AND PEPPERS MEXICAN-STYLE

MAKES 4 SERVINGS

1. Heat oil in large skillet over medium-high heat. Add green onions; cook and stir 2 minutes. Add pork; cook and stir 5 minutes or until browned. Add bell peppers and garlic; cook and stir 5 minutes or until bell peppers begin to soften.

2. Season with salt and black pepper. Add mushrooms, cumin, chili powder and chipotle chili powder, if desired; cook and stir 10 to 15 minutes or until pork is cooked through and vegetables are tender.

3. Serve with shredded cheese and sour cream.

2 tablespoons olive oil

1/2 cup chopped green onions

12 ounces lean pork, cut into 1/4-inch pieces

1 *each* red, yellow and green bell peppers, diced (about 2 cups)

1 teaspoon minced garlic

Salt and black pepper

1 cup sliced mushrooms

1 teaspoon ground cumin

1 teaspoon chili powder

1/2 teaspoon chipotle chili powder (optional)

1/4 cup (1 ounce) shredded Cheddar cheese

1/4 cup sour cream

Calories 271, Total Fat 16g, Carbs 9g, Net Carbs 6g, Fiber 3g, Protein 22g

TWO-CHEESE SAUSAGE PIZZA

MAKES 4 SERVINGS

1. Preheat oven to 400°F. Remove sausage from casings. Pat into 9-inch glass pie plate. Bake 10 minutes or until sausage is firm. Remove from oven and carefully pour off fat. Set aside.

2. Heat oil in large skillet. Add mushrooms, onion, bell pepper, salt, oregano and black pepper. Cook and stir over medium-high heat 10 minutes or until vegetables are very tender.

3. Combine pizza sauce and tomato paste in small bowl; stir until well blended. Spread over sausage crust. Spoon half of vegetables over tomato sauce. Sprinkle with Parmesan and mozzarella cheeses. Top with remaining vegetables. Sprinkle with olives. Bake 8 to 10 minutes or until cheese melts.

1 pound sweet Italian turkey sausage

1 tablespoon olive oil

2 cups sliced mushrooms

1 small red onion, thinly sliced

1 small green bell pepper, cut into thin strips

¼ teaspoon salt

¼ teaspoon dried oregano

¼ teaspoon black pepper

½ cup pizza sauce

2 tablespoons tomato paste

½ cup shredded Parmesan cheese

1 cup (4 ounces) shredded mozzarella cheese

8 pitted black olives

Calories 507, Total Fat 43g, Carbs 11g, Net Carbs 8g, Fiber 3g, Protein 27g

GRILLED STRIP STEAKS WITH FRESH CHIMICHURRI

MAKES 4 SERVINGS

1. For chimichurri, combine basil, oil, parsley, cilantro, lemon juice, garlic, 1/2 teaspoon salt, orange peel, coriander and 1/8 teaspoon pepper in food processor or blender; process until smooth.

2. Oil grid. Prepare grill for direct cooking. Sprinkle both sides of steaks with remaining 3/4 teaspoon salt, cumin and remaining 1/4 teaspoon pepper.

3. Grill steaks, covered, over medium-high heat 8 to 10 minutes for medium rare (145°F) or to desired doneness, turning once. Serve with chimichurri.

1/2 cup packed fresh basil leaves

1/3 cup extra virgin olive oil

1/4 cup packed fresh parsley

2 tablespoons packed fresh cilantro

2 tablespoons fresh lemon juice

1 clove garlic

1 1/4 teaspoons salt, divided

1/2 teaspoon grated orange peel

1/4 teaspoon ground coriander

1/4 teaspoon plus 1/8 teaspoon black pepper, divided

4 bone-in strip steaks (8 ounces each), about 1 inch thick

3/4 teaspoon ground cumin

Calories 630, Total Fat 50g, Carbs 1g, Net Carbs 1g, Fiber 0g, Protein 43g

PEPPERCORN STEAKS

MAKES 4 SERVINGS

1. Combine oil, peppercorns, herbs and garlic in small bowl. Rub mixture on both sides of steaks. Place on plate; cover and refrigerate 30 to 60 minutes.

2. Prepare grill for direct cooking.

3. Grill steaks, uncovered, over medium heat 10 to 12 minutes for medium rare (145°F) to medium (160°F) or to desired doneness, turning once. Season with salt.

2 **tablespoons olive oil**

1 to 2 **teaspoons cracked pink or black peppercorns or ground black pepper**

1 **teaspoon dried herbs, such as rosemary, thyme or oregano**

1 **teaspoon minced garlic**

4 **boneless beef top loin (strip) or rib-eye steaks (6 ounces each)**

¼ **teaspoon salt**

Calories 272, Total Fat 15g, Carbs 1g, Net Carbs 0g, Fiber 1g, Protein 33g

FLANK STEAK WITH ITALIAN SALSA

MAKES 6 SERVINGS

1. Whisk oil and vinegar in medium bowl until well blended. Place steak in shallow dish. Spread garlic over steak; sprinkle with $1/2$ teaspoon salt and $1/2$ teaspoon pepper. Spoon 2 tablespoons oil mixture over steak. Marinate in refrigerator at least 20 minutes or up to 2 hours.

2. Add tomatoes, olives, basil, remaining $1/4$ teaspoon salt and $1/4$ teaspoon pepper to remaining 2 teaspoons vinegar mixture in bowl; mix well.

3. Prepare grill for direct cooking or preheat broiler. Remove steak from marinade; discard marinade. (Leave garlic on steak.)

4. Grill steak over medium-high heat 5 to 6 minutes per side for medium rare (145°F). Remove to cutting board; tent with foil and let stand 5 minutes. Cut steak diagonally across the grain into thin slices. Serve with tomato mixture.

- 2 tablespoons olive oil
- 2 teaspoons balsamic vinegar
- 1 flank steak ($1^1/2$ pounds)
- 1 tablespoon minced garlic
- $3/4$ teaspoon salt, divided
- $3/4$ teaspoon black pepper, divided
- 1 cup diced plum tomatoes
- $1/3$ cup chopped pitted kalamata olives
- 2 tablespoons chopped fresh basil

Calories 191, Total Fat 11g, Carbs 4g, Net Carbs 3g, Fiber 1g, Protein 18g

CHILI Á LA MEXICO
MAKES 6 SERVINGS

1. Brown beef in large deep skillet over medium-high heat 6 to 8 minutes, stirring to break up meat. Drain fat. Add onions and garlic; cook and stir 5 minutes or until onions are softened.

2. Stir in tomatoes with juice, tomato paste, chili powder, cumin, salt, ground red pepper and cloves, if desired. Bring to a boil over high heat. Reduce heat to low; cover and simmer 30 minutes, stirring occasionally. Ladle into bowls. Garnish with lime wedges.

2 pounds ground beef

2 cups finely chopped onions

2 cloves garlic, minced

1 can (28 ounces) whole tomatoes, undrained and coarsely chopped

1 can (6 ounces) tomato paste

1½ to 2 tablespoons chili powder

1 teaspoon ground cumin

¼ teaspoon salt

¼ teaspoon ground red pepper

¼ teaspoon ground cloves (optional)

Lime wedges (optional)

Calories 350, Total Fat 18g, Carbs 16g, Net Carbs 11g, Fiber 5g, Protein 30g

BEEF AND PEPPER KABOBS

MAKES 4 SERVINGS

1. Slice steak into 16 (¼-inch) strips; place in glass bowl. Whisk garlic, soy sauce, vinegar, mustard, oil and black pepper in small bowl. Stir half of mixture into beef. Cover and refrigerate 2 to 3 hours, stirring occasionally. Cover remaining marinade and refrigerate.

2. Prepare grill for direct cooking. Core and seed bell peppers. Cut each into 12 chunks; thread onto 4 skewers.* Grill 5 to 7 minutes per side or until well browned and tender. Grill green onions 3 to 5 minutes or until well browned on both sides. Stir broth into reserved marinade. Brush bell peppers and green onions lightly with marinade once during grilling.

3. Thread 4 beef strips onto 4 skewers. Grill 2 minutes per side, basting once per side with marinade. To serve, coarsely chop green onions. Remove bell peppers and beef from skewers; sprinkle with green onions.

If using wooden skewers, soak in water 25 to 30 minutes before using to prevent burning.

8 ounces sirloin steak

1 clove garlic, minced

2 teaspoons soy sauce

2 teaspoons red wine vinegar

1½ teaspoons Dijon mustard

1 teaspoon olive oil

⅛ teaspoon black pepper

2 small bell peppers, green, red, yellow or orange

4 large green onions

1 tablespoon chicken broth or water

Calories 105, Total Fat 4g, Carbs 4g, Net Carbs 3g, Fiber 1g, Protein 14g

BEEF TENDERLOIN WITH SPICE RUB

MAKES 8 SERVINGS

1. Combine onion powder, thyme, cumin, black pepper, allspice, salt and red pepper in small bowl. Sprinkle evenly over all sides of beef and pat to adhere. Wrap tightly in plastic wrap and refrigerate 24 hours.

2. Preheat oven to 400°F. Spray sheet pan with nonstick cooking spray. Spray large nonstick skillet with cooking spray; heat over medium-high heat. Add beef; cook 3 minutes. Turn and cook 2 minutes or until well browned.

3. Using a flat spatula, transfer beef to prepared sheet pan. Add water to skillet and cook 15 seconds, stirring to scrape up browned bits. Drizzle over beef. Bake, uncovered, 25 minutes or until meat thermometer registers 135°F or to desired degree of doneness. Cover tightly with foil and let stand 10 minutes.

4. Place beef on cutting board, slice and arrange on serving platter. Spoon pan drippings over beef.

1 tablespoon onion powder

2 teaspoons dried thyme

1 teaspoon ground cumin

1 teaspoon black pepper or lemon pepper

$^3/_4$ teaspoon ground allspice

$^1/_2$ teaspoon salt

$^1/_8$ teaspoon ground red pepper

2 pounds beef tenderloin

$^1/_4$ cup water

Calories 180, Total Fat 8g, Carbs 1g, Net Carbs 0g, Fiber 1g, Protein 25g

BACON AND ONION BRISKET

MAKES 6 SERVINGS

SLOW COOKER DIRECTIONS

1. Cook bacon in large skillet over medium-high heat 3 minutes. Transfer bacon to 5-quart slow cooker with slotted spoon.

2. Season brisket with salt and pepper. Sear brisket in hot bacon fat on all sides, turning as it browns. Transfer to slow cooker.

3. Reduce heat to medium. Add onions; cook and stir 3 to 5 minutes or until softened. Add to slow cooker. Pour in broth. Cover; cook on HIGH 6 to 8 hours or until meat is tender.

4. Transfer brisket to cutting board and let rest 10 minutes. Slice against the grain into thin slices; season with additional salt and pepper, if desired. Serve brisket with bacon, onions and cooking liquid.

6 slices bacon, cut crosswise into $\frac{1}{2}$-inch strips

1 flat-cut boneless beef brisket (about 2$\frac{1}{2}$ pounds)

Salt and black pepper

3 medium onions, sliced

2 cans (14 ounces each) beef broth

Calories 360, Total Fat 18g, Carbs 5g, Net Carbs 4g, Fiber 1g, Protein 45g

RIB-EYE STEAKS WITH CHILI BUTTER

MAKES 4 SERVINGS

1. Beat butter, chili powder, garlic, mustard and red pepper in medium bowl until smooth. Place mixture on sheet of waxed paper. Roll mixture back and forth into 6-inch log using waxed paper. If butter is too soft, refrigerate up to 30 minutes. Wrap with waxed paper; refrigerate at least 1 hour or up to 2 days.

2. Prepare grill for direct cooking. Rub black pepper evenly over both sides of steaks; season with salt.

3. Place steaks on grid over medium-high heat. Grill, covered, 8 to 10 minutes or until desired doneness, turning occasionally. Slice chili butter; serve with steak.

½ cup (1 stick) butter, softened

2 teaspoons chili powder

1 teaspoon minced garlic

1 teaspoon Dijon mustard

⅛ teaspoon ground red pepper or chipotle chili powder

1 teaspoon black pepper

4 beef rib-eye steaks

Salt

Calories 500, Total Fat 37g, Carbs 2g, Net Carbs 1g, Fiber 1g, Protein 40g

PORK CURRY OVER CAULIFLOWER COUSCOUS

MAKES 6 SERVINGS

1. Heat 2 tablespoons oil in large saucepan over medium heat. Add curry powder and garlic; cook and stir 1 to 2 minutes or until garlic is golden.

2. Add pork; cook and stir 5 to 7 minutes or until pork is barely pink in center. Add bell pepper and vinegar; cook and stir 3 minutes or until bell pepper is soft. Sprinkle with $1/2$ teaspoon salt.

3. Add water; bring to a boil. Reduce heat; simmer 30 to 45 minutes until liquid is reduced and pork is tender, adding additional water as needed and stirring occasionally.

4. Meanwhile, trim and core cauliflower; cut into equal pieces. Place in food processor. Pulse until cauliflower is in small uniform pieces about the size of cooked couscous. *Do not purée.*

5. Heat remaining 1 tablespoon oil in 12-inch nonstick skillet over medium heat. Add cauliflower and remaining $1/2$ teaspoon salt; cook and stir 5 minutes or until crisp-tender. *Do not overcook.* Serve pork curry over cauliflower.

3 **tablespoons olive oil, divided**

2 **tablespoons mild curry powder**

2 **teaspoons minced garlic**

$1^{1}/_{2}$ **pounds boneless pork (shoulder, loin or chops), cubed**

1 **red or green bell pepper, diced**

1 **tablespoon cider vinegar**

1 **teaspoon salt, divided**

2 **cups water**

1 **large head cauliflower**

Calories 267, Total Fat 15g, Carbs 7g, Net Carbs 2g, Fiber 5g, Protein 28g

TEXAS MEETS N.Y. STRIP STEAKS

MAKES 4 SERVINGS

1. Heat 2 tablespoons oil in medium skillet over medium heat. Add onion; cook and stir 15 to 20 minutes or until soft and golden brown.

2. Meanwhile, prepare grill for direct cooking. Rub steaks with remaining 1 tablespoon oil and garlic. Sprinkle pepper on both sides of steaks and season with salt.

3. Grill steaks over medium-high heat 10 to 12 minutes to at least 145°F or to desired degree of doneness, turning twice to obtain cross-hatch grill marks. Serve steaks with onion.

3 tablespoons olive oil, divided

1 medium onion, thinly sliced

4 strip steaks (6 to 8 ounces each)

2 teaspoons minced garlic

2 teaspoons black pepper

Salt

Calories 450, Total Fat 25g, Carbs 2g, Net Carbs 1, Fiber 1g, Protein 50g

STEAK DIANE WITH CREMINI MUSHROOMS

MAKES 2 SERVINGS

1. Spray large nonstick skillet with nonstick cooking spray; heat over medium-high heat. Add steaks; sprinkle with salt and pepper. Cook 3 minutes per side for medium rare (145°F) or to desired doneness. Transfer to plate; keep warm.

2. Spray same skillet with cooking spray; heat over medium heat. Add shallots; cook and stir 2 minutes. Add mushrooms; cook and stir 3 minutes. Add Worcestershire sauce and mustard; cook 1 minute, stirring frequently.

3. Return steaks and any accumulated juices to skillet; heat through, turning once. Transfer steaks to serving plates; top with mushroom mixture.

2 beef tenderloin steaks (4 ounces each), cut $3/4$ inch thick

$1/4$ teaspoon salt

$1/4$ teaspoon black pepper

$1/3$ cup sliced shallots or chopped onion

4 ounces cremini mushrooms, sliced *or* 1 (4-ounce) package sliced mixed wild mushrooms

$1^1/2$ tablespoons Worcestershire sauce

1 tablespoon Dijon mustard

Calories 239, Total Fat 9g, Carbs 10g, Net Carbs 9g, Fiber 1g, Protein 28g

POULTRY

POLLO DIAVOLO (DEVILED CHICKEN)

MAKES 4 TO 6 SERVINGS

1. Place chicken in large resealable food storage bag. Combine oil, lemon juice, garlic and red pepper flakes in small bowl. Pour mixture over chicken. Seal bag; turn to coat. Refrigerate at least 1 hour or up to 8 hours, turning once.

2. Prepare grill for direct cooking over medium-high heat. Drain chicken, reserving marinade. Place chicken on grid; brush with reserved marinade. Grill, covered, 8 minutes. Turn chicken; brush with remaining reserved marinade. Grill, covered, 8 to 10 minutes or until cooked through (165°F).

3. Meanwhile, combine butter, sage, thyme, salt and ground red pepper in small bowl; mix well. Transfer chicken to serving platter; spread herb butter over chicken. Serve with lemon wedges.

8 skinless bone-in chicken thighs (2$\frac{1}{2}$ to 3 pounds)

$\frac{1}{4}$ cup olive oil

3 tablespoons lemon juice

6 cloves garlic, minced

1 to 2 teaspoons red pepper flakes

3 tablespoons butter, softened

1 teaspoon dried or rubbed sage

1 teaspoon dried thyme

$\frac{3}{4}$ teaspoon coarse salt

$\frac{1}{4}$ teaspoon ground red pepper or black pepper

Lemon wedges

Calories 550, Total Fat 34g, Carbs 3g, Net Carbs 3g, Fiber 0g, Protein 56g

CHICKEN AND SHRIMP JAMBALAYA

MAKES 6 SERVINGS

1. Place rutabaga in food processor; pulse until chopped into rice-size pieces.

2. Bring 2 cups broth to a boil in medium saucepan. Add rutabaga; cook 5 to 7 minutes or until tender. Drain and return to saucepan; keep warm.

3. Meanwhile, combine salt, black pepper and red pepper in small bowl; sprinkle half of mixture over chicken. Heat oil in large nonstick skillet or Dutch oven over medium heat. Add chicken; cook without stirring 2 minutes or until golden. Turn chicken; cook 2 minutes. Transfer chicken to plate; set aside.

4. Add onion and bell peppers to same skillet; cook and stir 3 minutes or until onion is translucent. Add garlic; cook and stir 1 minute. Stir in chicken, tomato, shrimp, remaining pepper mixture and $1/2$ cup broth; bring to a boil. Reduce heat to low; cook 5 minutes or until shrimp are opaque.

5. Stir in parsley and rutabaga. Add additional broth if needed to moisten. Cook 3 minutes longer or until liquid is absorbed and jambalaya is hot.

1 medium rutabaga, peeled and cubed

$2^1/2$ to 3 cups chicken broth, divided

$3/4$ teaspoon salt

$1/8$ teaspoon black pepper

$1/8$ teaspoon ground red pepper

8 ounces boneless skinless chicken breast, cut into $1/2$-inch pieces

1 tablespoon vegetable oil

1 large onion, thinly sliced

1 each red, yellow and green bell pepper, thinly sliced

2 cloves garlic, minced

1 large tomato, chopped

6 ounces peeled and deveined medium shrimp

2 tablespoons chopped fresh parsley

Calories 147, Total Fat 4g, Carbs 14g, Net Carbs 11, Fiber 3g, Protein 14g

TURKEY MEATBALLS WITH SPAGHETTI SQUASH

MAKES 5 SERVINGS

1. Preheat broiler. Line baking sheet with foil; brush with oil. Beat egg in large bowl. Add turkey, onion, almond flour, parsley, 1 teaspoon salt, garlic powder, thyme, fennel seeds, black pepper and red pepper flakes; mix well. Shape mixture into 20 meatballs; place on prepared baking sheet.

2. Broil meatballs 4 to 5 minutes or until tops are browned. Turn meatballs; broil 4 minutes.

3. Split squash in half and remove seeds. Place in glass baking dish, cut sides down; add water. Microwave on HIGH 10 to 12 minutes or until fork-tender. Set aside to cool.

4. Meanwhile, combine tomatoes, broth, green onions, basil, oregano and remaining ¼ teaspoon salt in large skillet; bring to a simmer over medium heat. Add meatballs; stir to coat. Reduce heat to medium-low; cook 10 minutes.

5. Scrape squash into strands into serving bowls. Top with meatballs and sauce.

2 teaspoons olive oil

1 egg

1 pound ground turkey

½ cup finely chopped onion

¼ cup almond flour

2 tablespoons chopped fresh parsley

1¼ teaspoons salt, divided

1 teaspoon garlic powder

¾ teaspoon dried thyme

¼ teaspoon fennel seeds

¼ teaspoon black pepper

⅛ teaspoon red pepper flakes

1 (12- to 16-ounce) spaghetti squash

¼ water

1 can (about 14 ounces) crushed tomatoes

¾ cup chicken broth

⅓ cup finely chopped green onions

½ teaspoon dried basil

½ teaspoon dried oregano

Calories 179, Total Fat 2g, Carbs 16g, Net Carbs 13g, Fiber 3g, Protein 25g

SPICED TARRAGON ROAST TURKEY BREAST

MAKES 6 SERVINGS

1. Preheat oven to 400°F. Whisk oil, orange peel, tarragon, cumin, allspice, cinnamon, ginger, salt, black pepper and red pepper in small bowl. Loosen skin from turkey and gently rub spice mixture under skin.

2. Spray broiler pan with nonstick cooking spray. Place turkey, skin side up, on prepared pan. Bake 1 hour 15 minutes or until meat reaches 165°F when tested with instant-read thermometer. Let stand 15 minutes. Remove and discard skin, leaving spice mixture on turkey. Thinly slice turkey.

2 tablespoons canola or corn oil

2 teaspoons grated orange peel

1½ teaspoons dried tarragon

1 teaspoon ground cumin

½ teaspoon ground allspice

½ teaspoon ground cinnamon

½ teaspoon ground ginger

½ teaspoon salt

½ teaspoon black pepper

¼ teaspoon ground red pepper

1 (2½-pound) bone-in turkey breast half, thawed if frozen

Calories 22, Total Fat 7g, Carbs 1g, Net Carbs 1g, Fiber 0g, Protein 36g

INDIAN-INSPIRED CHICKEN WITH RAITA

MAKES 6 TO 8 SERVINGS

1. Combine 1 cup yogurt, 2 cloves garlic, 1 teaspoon salt, coriander, ginger, turmeric, cinnamon, cumin and red pepper in medium bowl. Place chicken in large resealable food storage bag. Add yogurt mixture; turn to coat. Marinate in refrigerator 4 to 24 hours, turning occasionally.

2. Preheat broiler. Line baking sheet with foil. Place chicken on prepared baking sheet. Broil 6 inches from heat about 30 minutes or until cooked through (165°F), turning once.

3. Meanwhile for raita, combine cucumbers, 1/3 cup yogurt, cilantro, 1 clove garlic, 1/4 teaspoon salt and black pepper in small bowl. Serve with chicken.

1 cup plain yogurt

2 cloves garlic, minced

1 teaspoon salt

1 teaspoon ground coriander

1 teaspoon ground ginger

1/2 teaspoon ground turmeric

1/2 teaspoon ground cinnamon

1/2 teaspoon ground cumin

1/4 teaspoon ground red pepper

1 (5- to 6-pound) chicken, cut into 8 pieces (about 4 pounds chicken parts)

RAITA

2 medium cucumbers (about 1 pound), peeled, seeded and thinly sliced

1/3 cup plain yogurt

2 tablespoons chopped fresh cilantro

1 clove garlic, minced

1/4 teaspoon salt

1/8 teaspoon black pepper

Calories 625, Total Fat 43g, Carbs 8g, Net Carbs 7g, Fiber 1g, Protein 50g

SWISS, TOMATO AND TURKEY PATTY MELT

MAKES 4 SERVINGS

1. Combine turkey, salad dressing mix and green onion in medium bowl; mix well. Shape into 4 patties.

2. Spray large nonstick skillet with nonstick cooking spray; heat over medium heat. Add oil; tilt skillet to coat bottom evenly. Add patties. Cook 14 minutes or until cooked through (165°F), turning once.

3. Remove skillet from heat. Top each patty with cheese. Cover and let stand 2 to 3 minutes or until cheese melts. Top each patty with tomatoes.

1 pound ground turkey

½ (1-ounce) package ranch salad dressing mix

1 medium green onion, finely chopped

1 teaspoon olive oil

2 slices Swiss cheese, halved diagonally

1 medium tomato, diced

Calories 239, Total Fat 11g, Carbs 3g, Net Carbs 2g, Fiber 1g, Protein 28g

CHICKEN SATAY

MAKES 4 SERVINGS

1. Place chicken in large resealable food storage bag; add soy sauce. Seal bag; turn to coat. Marinate in refrigerator 45 minutes.

2. Meanwhile for peanut sauce, heat oil in large nonstick skillet over medium-high heat. Add onion and garlic; cook and stir 5 minutes or until golden brown. Stir in ginger; cook 30 seconds. Stir in peanut butter, water, ketchup, salt and pepper.

3. Reduce heat to low; cook until mixture is heated through. Transfer to blender and purée until smooth.

4. Preheat broiler. Spray broiler rack with nonstick cooking spray. Thread chicken strips onto 16 (8-inch) wooden skewers. Discard soy sauce. Broil 6 inches from heat 5 to 6 minutes or until just cooked through, turning once.

5. Serve with peanut sauce.

SATAY

16 **chicken tenders (about 2¹/₄ pounds)** *or* **4 boneless skinless chicken breasts cut into 16 thin strips**

¹/₂ **cup soy sauce**

PEANUT SAUCE

1 **tablespoon vegetable oil**

1 **onion, chopped**

2 **cloves garlic, minced**

2 **teaspoons ground ginger**

¹/₂ **cup peanut butter**

¹/₂ **cup water**

1¹/₂ **teaspoons ketchup**

¹/₄ **teaspoon salt**

¹/₈ **teaspoon black pepper**

Calories 558, Total Fat 24g, Carbs 15g, Net Carbs 13g, Fiber 2g, Protein 71g

PESTO-STUFFED GRILLED CHICKEN

MAKES 6 SERVINGS

1. Prepare grill with rectangular metal or foil drip pan. Bank briquettes on either side of drip pan for indirect cooking.

2. Meanwhile for pesto, place 1/2 cup basil, pine nuts, garlic, salt and pepper in food processor; process until basil is minced. With motor running, add 3 tablespoons oil in slow, steady stream until smooth paste forms, scraping down side of bowl once. Add cheese; process until well blended.

3. Remove giblets from chicken cavity. Loosen skin over breast of chicken by pushing fingers between skin and meat, taking care not to tear skin. Do not loosen skin over wings and drumsticks. Using rubber spatula or small spoon, spread pesto under breast skin; massage skin to evenly spread pesto. Combine remaining 2 tablespoons oil and lemon juice in small bowl; brush over skin. Tuck wings under back; tie legs together with kitchen string.

4. Place chicken, breast side up, on grid directly over drip pan. Grill, covered, over medium-low heat 1 hour 10 minutes to 1 hour 30 minutes or until instant-read thermometer inserted into thickest part of thigh not touching bone registers 185°F, adding 4 to 9 briquettes to both sides of the fire after 45 minutes to maintain medium-low heat. Transfer chicken to carving board; tent with foil. Let stand 15 minutes before carving.

1/2 cup packed fresh basil leaves

2 tablespoons pine nuts or walnuts, toasted*

2 cloves garlic

1/4 teaspoon salt

1/4 teaspoon black pepper

5 tablespoons extra virgin olive oil, divided

1/4 cup grated Parmesan cheese

1 fresh or thawed frozen roasting chicken or capon (6 to 7 pounds)

2 tablespoons fresh lemon juice

To toast pine nuts, spread in single layer in heavy skillet. Cook over medium heat 1 to 2 minutes, stirring frequently, until nuts are lightly browned. Cool before using.

Calories 618, Total Fat 49g, Carbs 1g, Net Carbs 0g, Fiber 1g, Protein 40g

FARM-RAISED CATFISH WITH BACON AND HORSERADISH

MAKES 6 SERVINGS

1. Preheat oven to 350°F. Grease large baking dish. Arrange fish in single layer in prepared dish.

2. Melt butter in small skillet over medium-high heat. Add onion; cook and stir until softened. Combine cream cheese, broth, horseradish, mustard, salt and pepper in small bowl; stir in onion. Spread over fish and top with crumbled bacon.

3. Bake 30 minutes or until fish begins to flake when tested with fork. Serve immediately.

6 farm-raised catfish fillets (4 to 5 ounces each)

2 tablespoons butter

1/4 cup chopped onion

1 package (8 ounces) cream cheese, softened

1/4 cup vegetable or chicken broth

2 tablespoons prepared horseradish

1 tablespoon Dijon mustard

1/2 teaspoon salt

1/8 teaspoon black pepper

4 slices bacon, crisp-cooked and crumbled

Calories 380, Total Fat 30g, Carbs 4g, Net Carbs 4g, Fiber 0g, Protein 22g

CRAB SPINACH SALAD WITH TARRAGON DRESSING

MAKES 4 SERVINGS

1. Combine crabmeat, tomatoes, cucumber and onion in medium bowl. Combine mayonnaise, sour cream, parsley, milk, tarragon, garlic and hot pepper sauce in small bowl.

2. Line four salad plates with spinach. Place crabmeat mixture on spinach; drizzle with dressing.

12 ounces coarsely flaked cooked crabmeat *or* 2 packages (6 ounces each) frozen crabmeat, thawed and drained

1 cup chopped tomatoes

1 cup sliced cucumber

1/3 cup sliced red onion

1/4 cup mayonnaise

1/4 cup sour cream

1/4 cup chopped fresh parsley

2 tablespoons milk

2 teaspoons chopped fresh tarragon *or* 1/2 teaspoon dried tarragon

1 clove garlic, minced

1/4 teaspoon hot pepper sauce

8 cups fresh spinach

Calories 170, Total Fat 4g, Carbs 14g, Net Carbs 10g, Fiber 4g, Protein 22g

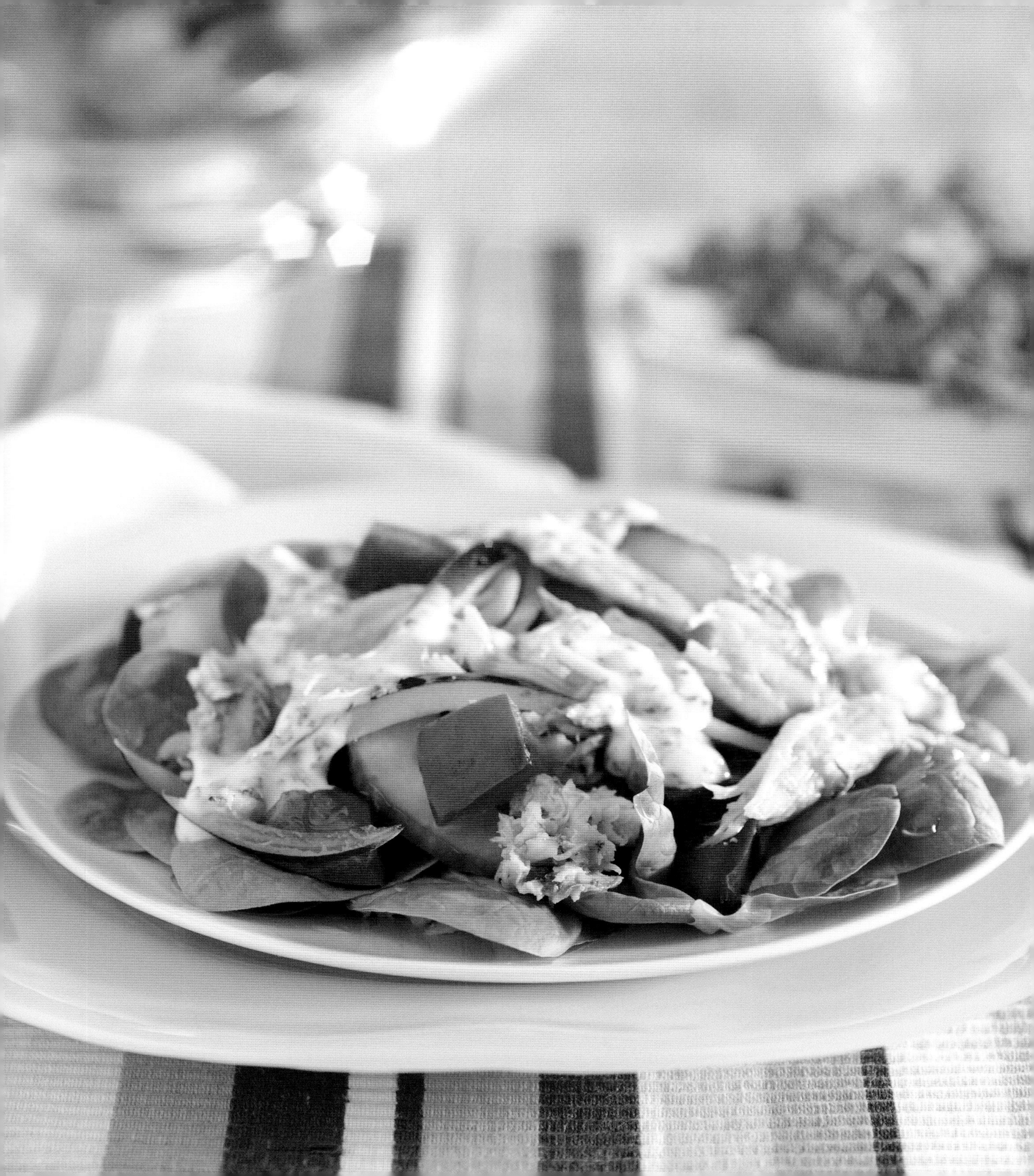

GRILLED SCALLOPS AND VEGETABLES WITH CILANTRO SAUCE

MAKES 4 SERVINGS

1. Spray grid with nonstick cooking spray; prepare grill for direct cooking. Heat chili oil and sesame oil in small saucepan over medium-low heat. Add green onion; cook about 15 seconds or just until fragrant. Add ginger; cook 1 minute.

2. Add broth; bring mixture to a boil. Cook until liquid is reduced by half. Cool slightly. Place mixture in blender or food processor with cilantro; blend until smooth.

3. Thread scallops and vegetables onto 4 (12-inch) skewers.* Grill about 8 minutes per side or until scallops turn opaque. Serve hot with cilantro sauce.

If using wooden skewers, soak in water 25 to 30 minutes before using to prevent burning.

1 teaspoon hot chili oil

1 teaspoon dark sesame oil

1 green onion, chopped

1 tablespoon finely chopped fresh ginger

1 cup chicken broth

1 cup chopped fresh cilantro

1 pound raw or thawed frozen sea scallops

2 medium zucchini, cut into $1/2$-inch slices

2 medium yellow squash, cut into $1/2$-inch slices

1 medium yellow onion, cut into wedges

8 large mushrooms

Calories 194, Total Fat 7g, Carbs 11g, Net Carbs 8g, Fiber 3g, Protein 23g

GRILLED CHINESE SALMON

MAKES 4 SERVINGS

1. Combine soy sauce, sherry and garlic in shallow dish. Add salmon; turn to coat. Cover; marinate in refrigerator at least 30 minutes or up to 2 hours.

2. Oil grid. Prepare grill for direct cooking. Remove salmon from dish, reserving marinade. Grill fish, skin side down, over high heat 10 minutes or until center is opaque. Baste with reserved marinade after 5 minutes of cooking; discard any remaining marinade. To broil, place salmon on oiled broiler rack or baking sheet. Broil 10 minutes or until center is opaque. Sprinkle with cilantro.

3 tablespoons soy sauce

2 tablespoons dry sherry

2 cloves garlic, minced

4 salmon fillet pieces or steaks (about 5 ounces each)

2 tablespoons finely chopped fresh cilantro

Calories 223, Total Fat 12g, Carbs 1g, Net Carbs 0g, Fiber 1g, Protein 24g

PAN-SEARED HALIBUT STEAKS WITH AVOCADO SALSA

MAKES 4 SERVINGS

1. Combine 2 tablespoons salsa and ¼ teaspoon salt in small bowl; spread over both sides of fish.

2. Heat large nonstick skillet over medium heat. Add fish; cook 4 to 5 minutes per side or until fish is opaque in center.

3. Meanwhile, combine remaining 2 tablespoons salsa, ¼ teaspoon salt, tomato, avocado and cilantro, if desired, in small bowl. Mix well and spoon over cooked fish. Garnish with lime wedges.

4 tablespoons chipotle salsa, divided

½ teaspoon salt, divided

4 small (4 to 5 ounces) *or* 2 large (8 to 10 ounces) halibut steaks, cut ¾ inch thick

½ cup diced tomato

½ ripe avocado, diced

2 tablespoons chopped fresh cilantro (optional)

Lime wedges (optional)

Calories 169, Total Fat 7g, Carbs 2g, Net Carbs 0g, Fiber 4g, Protein 25g

SKILLET FISH WITH LEMON TARRAGON BUTTER

MAKES 2 SERVINGS

1. Combine butter, 2 teaspoons lemon juice, lemon peel, mustard, tarragon and salt in small bowl; mix well.

2. Spray 12-inch nonstick skillet with nonstick cooking spray; heat over medium heat. Drizzle fish with remaining 2 teaspoons lemon juice; sprinkle one side of each fillet with paprika.

3. Place fish in skillet, paprika side down; cook 3 minutes. Gently turn and cook 3 minutes longer or until fish is opaque in center and begins to flake when tested with fork. Top with butter mixture.

- 2 teaspoons butter, melted
- 4 teaspoons lemon juice, divided
- ½ teaspoon grated lemon peel
- ¼ teaspoon Dijon mustard
- ¼ teaspoon dried tarragon
- ¼ teaspoon salt
- 2 lean white fish fillets (4 ounces each), such as orange roughy or sole, rinsed and patted dry
- ¼ teaspoon paprika

Calories 125, Total Fat 3g, Carbs 1g, Net Carbs 0g, Fiber 1g, Protein 22g

SHRIMP AND TOMATO STIR-FRY

MAKES 4 SERVINGS

1. Combine olives, tomatoes, basil, $1/8$ teaspoon salt and pepper in medium bowl. Toss gently to blend.

2. Spray 12-inch nonstick skillet with nonstick cooking spray; heat over medium heat. Add shrimp, garlic and red pepper flakes; cook and stir 3 minutes or until shrimp are opaque. Remove from skillet; set aside.

3. Spray same skillet with cooking spray; heat over medium-high heat. Add zucchini, onion and remaining $1/4$ teaspoon salt; cook and stir 5 minutes or until edges of vegetables begin to brown.

4. Add tomato mixture and shrimp to skillet; cook and stir 1 minute until heated through.

20 kalamata olives, pitted and coarsely chopped

1 cup cherry tomatoes, halved

$1/4$ cup chopped fresh basil

$1/4$ teaspoon plus $1/8$ teaspoon salt, divided

$1/4$ teaspoon black pepper

1 pound peeled medium raw shrimp

1 clove garlic, minced

$1/8$ teaspoon red pepper flakes

1 medium zucchini, quartered lengthwise, then cut crosswise into 2-inch pieces

1 medium onion, cut into 8 wedges

Calories 165, Total Fat 5g, Carbs 7g, Net Carbs 6g, Fiber 1g, Protein 24g

HAZELNUT-COATED SALMON STEAKS

MAKES 4 SERVINGS

1. Preheat oven to 375°F. Spread hazelnuts on ungreased baking sheet; bake 8 minutes or until lightly browned. Immediately transfer nuts to clean, dry dish towel. Fold towel over nuts; rub vigorously to remove as much of skins as possible. Finely chop hazelnuts in food processor or with knife.

2. *Increase oven temperature to 450°F.* Place salmon in single layer in baking dish. Combine apple butter, mustard and thyme in small bowl; season with salt and pepper. Top with hazelnuts, pressing to adhere.

3. Bake 14 to 16 minutes or until salmon begins to flake when tested with fork.

¼ cup hazelnuts

4 salmon steaks (about 5 ounces each)

1 tablespoon apple butter

1 tablespoon Dijon mustard

¼ teaspoon dried thyme

Salt and black pepper

Calories 350, Total Fat 23g, Carbs 2g, Net Carbs 1g, Fiber 1g, Protein 30g

MUSTARD-GRILLED RED SNAPPER

MAKES 4 SERVINGS

1. Spray grid with nonstick cooking spray. Prepare grill for direct cooking.

2. Combine mustard, vinegar and red pepper in small bowl; mix well. Brush mixture all over fish.

3. Grill fish, covered, over medium-high heat 8 minutes or until fish begins to flake easily when tested with fork, turning once. Serve immediately.

½ cup Dijon mustard

1 tablespoon red wine vinegar

1 teaspoon ground red pepper

4 red snapper fillets (about 6 ounces each)

Calories 210, Total Fat 5g, Carbs 4g, Net Carbs 3g, Fiber 1g, Protein 37g

MESQUITE-GRILLED SALMON FILLETS
MAKES 4 SERVINGS

1. Cover 1 cup mesquite chips with cold water in small bowl; soak 20 to 30 minutes. Spray grid with nonstick cooking spray. Prepare grill for direct cooking.

2. Combine oil and garlic in small microwavable bowl. Microwave on HIGH 1 minute or until garlic is tender. Add lemon juice, lemon peel, dill weed, thyme, salt and pepper; whisk until blended. Brush half of mixture all over skinless sides of salmon.

3. Drain mesquite chips; sprinkle chips over coals or place on a piece of foil on grid for gas grill. Place salmon, skin side up, on grid. Grill, covered, over medium-high heat 4 to 5 minutes; turn and brush with remaining lemon mixture. Grill 4 to 5 minutes or until salmon flakes when tested with fork.

- 2 tablespoons olive oil
- 1 clove garlic, minced
- 2 tablespoons lemon juice
- 1 teaspoon grated lemon peel
- 1/2 teaspoon dried dill weed
- 1/2 teaspoon dried thyme
- 1/4 teaspoon salt
- 1/4 teaspoon black pepper
- 4 salmon fillets (about 5 ounces each)

Calories 322, Total Fat 22g, Carbs 1g, Net Carbs 0g, Fiber 1g, Protein 28g

SHRIMP AND VEGGIE SKILLET TOSS

MAKES 4 SERVINGS

1. Whisk soy sauce, lime juice, oil, ginger and red pepper flakes in small bowl; set aside.

2. Spray large nonstick skillet with nonstick cooking spray; heat over medium-high heat. Add shrimp; cook and stir 3 minutes or until shrimp are opaque. Remove from skillet.

3. Spray same skillet with cooking spray. Add zucchini; cook and stir 4 to 6 minutes or just until crisp-tender. Add green onions and tomatoes; cook 1 to 2 minutes. Add shrimp; cook 1 minute. Transfer to large bowl.

4. Add soy sauce mixture to skillet; bring to a boil. Remove from heat. Stir in shrimp and vegetables; toss gently.

$1/4$ cup soy sauce

2 tablespoons lime juice

1 tablespoon dark sesame oil

1 teaspoon grated fresh ginger

$1/8$ teaspoon red pepper flakes

32 medium raw shrimp (about 8 ounces), peeled, deveined, rinsed and patted dry

2 medium zucchini, cut in half lengthwise and thinly sliced

6 green onions, trimmed and halved lengthwise

12 grape tomatoes

Calories 147, Total Fat 5g, Carbs 13g, Net Carbs 11g, Fiber 2g, Protein 15g

PAN-SEARED SCALLOPS WITH MUSHROOMS AND LEEKS

MAKES 4 SERVINGS

1. Melt 1 tablespoon butter in large nonstick skillet over medium-high heat. Sprinkle scallops with 1/4 teaspoon salt and 1/8 teaspoon pepper. Add to skillet; cook 2 to 3 minutes per side or until browned and opaque. (Cook in batches if necessary to prevent overcrowding.) Remove scallops to plate; keep warm.

2. Melt remaining 2 tablespoons butter in same skillet over medium-high heat. Add mushrooms; cook 3 to 4 minutes or just until mushrooms begin to brown slightly. Add leek and garlic; cook and stir 3 to 4 minutes or until leek is tender. Add broth; cook about 2 minutes or until almost evaporated. Stir in cream; bring to a boil and cook 1 minute. Add cheese, remaining 1/4 teaspoon salt and 1/8 teaspoon pepper; cook and stir about 30 seconds or until cheese melts.

3. Return scallops to skillet; cook 1 to 2 minutes or until heated through. Serve immediately.

3 tablespoons butter, divided

1 1/2 pounds sea scallops, patted dry

1/2 teaspoon salt, divided

1/4 teaspoon black pepper, divided

1 package (8 ounces) sliced mushrooms

1 medium leek, white and light green parts only, cut in half crosswise and very thinly sliced lengthwise

2 cloves garlic, minced

1/2 cup vegetable or chicken broth

1/3 cup whipping cream

1/4 cup (1 ounce) shredded Dubliner cheese

Calories 320, Total Fat 19g, Carbs 12g, Net Carbs 11g, Fiber 1g, Protein 24g

GRILLED TILAPIA WITH ZESTY MUSTARD SAUCE

MAKES 4 SERVINGS

1. Prepare grill for direct cooking over high heat.

2. Stir together oil, mustard, lemon peel, Worcestershire sauce, $1/4$ teaspoon salt and pepper in small bowl until well blended. Set aside.

3. Rinse fish and pat dry with paper towels. Sprinkle both sides of fish with paprika and remaining $1/4$ teaspoon salt. Lightly spray grill basket with nonstick cooking spray; place fish in basket. Grill, covered, 3 minutes. Turn and grill, covered, 2 to 3 minutes, or until fish flakes easily when tested with fork. Transfer to platter.

4. Squeeze one lemon wedge over each fillet. Spread butter mixture evenly over fish; garnish with parsley.

1 tablespoon olive oil

1 teaspoon Dijon mustard

$1/2$ teaspoon grated lemon peel

$1/2$ teaspoon Worcestershire sauce

$1/2$ teaspoon salt, divided

$1/4$ teaspoon black pepper

4 tilapia fillets (about 4 ounces each)

$1^1/2$ teaspoons paprika

$1/2$ medium lemon, quartered

2 tablespoons minced fresh parsley (optional)

Calories 136, Total Fat 5g, Carbs 1g, Net Carbs 0g, Fiber 1g, Protein 23g

CHIPOTLE SHRIMP WITH SQUASH RIBBONS

MAKES 4 SERVINGS

1. Place garlic, chipotle pepper, adobo sauce and water in food processor; process until smooth.

2. Using a vegetable peeler, shave squash into ribbons (discarding the seedy middle). Set aside.

3. Heat oil in large skillet over high heat; add onion and bell pepper. Cook and stir 1 minute. Add shrimp and chipotle mixture; cook 2 minutes. Add squash; cook and stir 1 to 2 minutes or until shrimp are opaque and squash are heated through and slightly wilted. Garnish with lime wedges.

2 cloves garlic

1 canned chipotle pepper in adobo sauce, plus 1 teaspoon sauce

2 tablespoons water

2 medium zucchini

2 medium yellow squash

1 teaspoon olive oil

1 small onion, diced

1 medium red bell pepper, cut into strips

8 ounces raw medium shrimp, peeled

Lime wedges (optional)

Calories 139, Total Fat 3g, Carbs 13g, Net Carbs 10g, Fiber 3g, Protein 14g

LEMON ROSEMARY SHRIMP AND VEGETABLE SOUVLAKI

MAKES 4 KABOBS

1. Prepare grill for direct cooking. Spray grid or grill pan with nonstick cooking spray.

2. Spray 4 (12-inch) wooden* or metal skewers with cooking spray. Alternately thread shrimp, zucchini, bell pepper and green onions onto skewers. Spray skewers lightly with cooking spray.

3. Combine oil, lemon juice, lemon peel, garlic, salt, rosemary and red pepper flakes in small bowl; mix well.

4. Grill skewers over high heat 2 minutes per side. Remove to serving platter; drizzle with sauce.

If using wooden skewers, soak in water 25 to 30 minutes before using to prevent burning.

8 ounces large raw shrimp, peeled and deveined

1 medium zucchini, halved lengthwise and cut into $\frac{1}{2}$-inch slices

$\frac{1}{2}$ medium red bell pepper, cut into 1-inch pieces

8 green onions, trimmed and cut into 2-inch pieces

SAUCE

2 tablespoons extra virgin olive oil

2 tablespoons lemon juice

2 teaspoons grated lemon peel

2 medium cloves garlic, minced

$\frac{1}{2}$ teaspoon salt

$\frac{1}{2}$ teaspoon fresh rosemary

$\frac{1}{8}$ teaspoon red pepper flakes

Calories 147, Total Fat 8g, Carbs 7g, Net Carbs 5g, Fiber 2g, Protein 13g

SALMON SALAD WITH BASIL VINAIGRETTE

MAKES 4 SERVINGS

1. For vinaigrette, whisk 3 tablespoons oil, vinegar, basil, garlic, chives, 1/4 teaspoon salt and 1/4 teaspoon pepper in small bowl until well blended.

2. Preheat oven to 400°F or prepare grill for direct cooking.

3. Combine 3 inches water and 1 teaspoon salt in large saucepan; bring to a boil over high heat. Add asparagus; simmer 6 to 8 minutes or until crisp-tender; drain and set aside.

4. Brush salmon with remaining 1 1/2 teaspoons oil. Sprinkle with remaining 1/4 teaspoon salt and 1/4 teaspoon pepper. Place fish in shallow baking pan; cook 11 to 13 minutes or until center is opaque. (Or grill on well-oiled grid over medium-high heat 4 or 5 minutes per side or until center is opaque.)

5. Remove skin from salmon; break into bite-size pieces. Arrange salmon over asparagus; drizzle with vinaigrette. Serve with lemon wedges.

3 tablespoons plus 1 1/2 teaspoons extra virgin olive oil, divided

1 tablespoon white wine vinegar

1 tablespoon minced fresh basil

1 clove garlic, minced

1 teaspoon minced fresh chives

1 1/2 teaspoons salt, divided

1/2 teaspoon black pepper, divided

1 pound asparagus, trimmed

1 pound salmon fillet

4 lemon wedges

Calories 332, Total Fat 24g, Carbs 5g, Net Carbs 3g, Fiber 2g, Protein 25g

TILAPIA WITH SPINACH AND FETA

MAKES 2 SERVINGS

1. Preheat oven to 350°F. Spray baking sheet with nonstick cooking spray.

2. Heat oil in medium skillet over medium-low heat. Add garlic; cook and stir 30 seconds. Add spinach; cook just until wilted, stirring occasionally.

3. Arrange tilapia on prepared baking sheet; sprinkle with pepper. Place one piece of cheese on each fillet; top with spinach mixture.

4. Fold one end of each fillet up and over filling; secure with toothpick. Repeat with opposite end of each fillet.

5. Bake 20 minutes or until fish begins to flake when tested with fork.

1 teaspoon olive oil

1 clove garlic, minced

4 cups baby spinach

2 skinless tilapia fillets or other mild white fish (4 ounces each)

1/4 teaspoon black pepper

2 ounces feta cheese, cut into 2 (3-inch) pieces

Calories 193, Total Fat 9g, Carbs 3g, Net Carbs 2g, Fiber 1g, Protein 26g

SZECHUAN TUNA STEAKS

MAKES 4 SERVINGS

1. Place tuna in single layer in large shallow glass dish. Combine sherry, soy sauce, sesame oil, chili oil and garlic in small bowl. Reserve 1/4 cup soy sauce mixture at room temperature. Pour remaining soy sauce mixture over tuna. Cover; marinate in refrigerator 40 minutes, turning once.

2. Spray grid with nonstick cooking spray. Prepare grill for direct cooking.

3. Drain tuna, discarding marinade. Grill tuna, uncovered, over medium-hot coals 6 minutes or until tuna is seared, but still feels somewhat soft in center,* turning halfway through grilling time. Transfer tuna to cutting board. Cut each tuna steak into thin slices; arrange slices onto serving plates. Drizzle with reserved soy sauce mixture; garnish with cilantro.

Tuna becomes dry and tough if overcooked. Cook to medium doneness for best results.

- 4 tuna steaks (6 ounces each), cut 1 inch thick
- 1/4 cup dry sherry or sake
- 1/4 cup soy sauce
- 1 tablespoon dark sesame oil
- 1 teaspoon hot chili oil *or* 1/4 teaspoon red pepper flakes
- 1 clove garlic, minced
- 3 tablespoons chopped fresh cilantro (optional)

Calories 284, Total Fat 11g, Carbs 2g, Net Carbs 1g, Fiber 1g, Protein 40g

VEGETABLES & SIDES

BRUSSELS SPROUTS WITH BACON AND BUTTER

MAKES 4 SERVINGS

1. Preheat oven to 375°F. Cook bacon in medium skillet until almost crisp. Drain on paper towel-lined plate; set aside. Reserve 1 tablespoon drippings for cooking brussels sprouts.

2. Place brussels sprouts on large baking sheet. Drizzle with reserved bacon drippings and sprinkle with 1/4 teaspoon salt and 1/4 teaspoon pepper; toss to coat. Spread in single layer on baking sheet.

3. Roast 30 minutes or until brussels sprouts are browned and crispy, stirring once.

4. Place brussels sprouts in large bowl; stir in butter until completely coated. Stir in bacon; season with additional salt and pepper.

6 slices thick-cut bacon, cut into 1/2-inch pieces

1 1/2 pounds brussels sprouts (about 24 medium), halved

1/4 teaspoon salt

1/4 teaspoon black pepper

2 tablespoons butter, softened

Calories 220, Total Fat 15g, Carbs 15g, Net Carbs 8g, Fiber 7g, Protein 10g

WEDGE SALAD

MAKES 4 SERVINGS

1. For dressing, combine mayonnaise, buttermilk, 1/2 cup cheese, garlic, sugar, onion powder, salt and pepper in food processor or blender; process until smooth.

2. For salad, cut lettuce into quarters through stem end; remove stem from each wedge. Place wedges on individual serving plates; top with dressing. Sprinkle with tomato, onion, remaining 1/2 cup cheese and bacon.

DRESSING

- 3/4 cup mayonnaise
- 1/2 cup buttermilk
- 1 cup crumbled blue cheese, divided
- 1 clove garlic, minced
- 1/2 teaspoon sugar
- 1/8 teaspoon onion powder
- 1/8 teaspoon salt
- 1/8 teaspoon ground black pepper

SALAD

- 1 head iceberg lettuce
- 1 large tomato, diced (about 1 cup)
- 1/2 small red onion, cut into thin rings
- 1/2 cup crumbled crisp-cooked bacon (6 to 8 slices)

Calories 460, Total Fat 42g, Carbs 9g, Net Carbs 7g, Fiber 2g, Protein 13g

CAULIFLOWER WITH ONION BUTTER

MAKES 8 TO 10 SERVINGS

1. Melt ¼ cup butter in medium skillet over medium heat. Add onion; cook and stir about 20 minutes or until onion is brown.

2. Meanwhile, place cauliflower and water in microwavable bowl. Microwave on HIGH 8 minutes or until crisp-tender; drain, if necessary.

3. Add remaining ¼ cup butter to skillet with onion; cook and stir until butter is melted. Pour over cooked cauliflower; serve immediately.

½ cup (1 stick) butter, divided

1 cup diced onion

1 large head cauliflower, broken into florets

½ cup water

Calories 108, Total Fat 11g, Carbs 2g, Net Carbs 1g, Fiber 1g, Protein 1g

BLT CHICKEN SALAD FOR TWO

MAKES 2 SERVINGS

1. Prepare grill for direct cooking.

2. Brush chicken with ¼ cup mayonnaise; sprinkle with pepper. Grill over medium heat 5 to 7 minutes per side or until no longer pink in center. Cool slightly; cut into thin strips.

3. Arrange lettuce on serving plates. Top with chicken, tomato, bacon and egg. Serve with additional mayonnaise, if desired.

2 boneless skinless chicken breasts

¼ cup mayonnaise

½ teaspoon black pepper

4 large lettuce leaves

1 large tomato, seeded and diced

3 slices bacon, crisp-cooked and crumbled

1 hard-cooked egg, chopped

Additional mayonnaise or salad dressing (optional)

Calories 426, Total Fat 30g, Carbs 5g, Net Carbs 4g, Fiber 1g, Protein 34g

ASPARAGUS WITH RED ONION, BASIL AND ALMONDS

MAKES 4 SERVINGS

1. Melt butter in medium skillet over medium heat. Add onion; cover and cook 5 minutes or until wilted. Uncover; cook 4 to 5 minutes until onion is tender and golden brown, stirring occasionally.

2. Place asparagus and broth in medium saucepan. Cover; bring to a boil over high heat. Reduce heat; simmer 4 minutes. Uncover; stir in onion. Cook about 2 minutes or until asparagus is crisp-tender and most liquid is evaporated. Stir in basil, salt and pepper. Transfer to serving plate. Sprinkle with almonds.

- 2 teaspoons butter
- 1/2 cup thinly sliced red onion, separated into rings
- 1 pound fresh asparagus, trimmed and cut into 1 1/2-inch pieces
- 1/4 cup chicken broth
- 2 tablespoons chopped fresh basil
- 1/4 teaspoon salt
- 1/4 teaspoon black pepper
- 2 tablespoons sliced almonds, toasted*

To toast almonds, place in nonstick skillet. Cook and stir over medium-low heat until nuts begin to brown, about 5 minutes. Remove immediately to plate to cool.

Calories 60, Total Fat 4g, Carbs 6g, Net Carbs 4g, Fiber 2g, Protein 3g

SAUTÉED KALE WITH MUSHROOMS AND BACON

MAKES 4 SERVINGS

1. Cook bacon in large heavy skillet over medium heat 5 minutes.

2. Add shallots; cook and stir 3 minutes. Add mushrooms; cook and stir 8 minutes.

3. Add kale and water; cover and cook 5 minutes. Uncover; cook and stir 5 minutes or until kale is crisp-tender. Season with pepper.

- 1 slice bacon, chopped
- ½ cup sliced shallots
- 1 package (4 ounces) sliced mixed exotic mushrooms *or* 8 ounces cremini mushrooms, sliced
- 10 cups loosely packed torn fresh kale leaves (about 8 ounces), stems removed
- 2 tablespoons water
- ½ teaspoon black pepper

Calories 90, Total Fat 4g, Carbs 11g, Net Carbs 8g, Fiber 3g, Protein 4g

STEAKHOUSE CHOPPED SALAD

MAKES 10 SERVINGS

1. For dressing, whisk salad dressing mix, vinegar and mustard in small bowl. Slowly add oil, whisking until well blended. Set aside until ready to use. (Dressing can be made up to 1 week in advance; refrigerate in jar with tight-fitting lid.)

2. For salad, combine lettuce, artichokes, avocado, cheese, eggs, tomato, onion and bacon in large bowl. Add dressing; toss to coat.

DRESSING

- 1 package (1 ounce) Italian salad dressing mix
- ⅓ cup white balsamic vinegar
- ¼ cup Dijon mustard
- ⅔ cup extra virgin olive oil

SALAD

- 1 medium head iceberg lettuce, chopped
- 1 medium head romaine lettuce, chopped
- 1 can (about 14 ounces) artichoke hearts, quartered lengthwise then sliced crosswise
- 1 large avocado, diced
- 1½ cups crumbled blue cheese
- 2 hard-cooked eggs, chopped
- 1 ripe tomato, chopped
- ½ small red onion, finely chopped
- 12 slices bacon, crisp-cooked and crumbled

Calories 344, Total Fat 26g, Carbs 16g, Net Carbs 12g, Fiber 4g, Protein 12g

COLORFUL COLESLAW

MAKES 6 SERVINGS

1. Combine cabbage, bell pepper, jicama, green onions and cilantro in large bowl.

2. Whisk oil, lime juice, salt and black pepper in small bowl until well blended. Pour over vegetables; toss to coat. Cover and refrigerate 2 to 6 hours for flavors to blend.

$\frac{1}{4}$ head green cabbage, shredded or thinly sliced

$\frac{1}{4}$ head red cabbage, shredded or thinly sliced

1 small yellow or orange bell pepper, thinly sliced

1 small jicama, peeled and julienned

$\frac{1}{4}$ cup thinly sliced green onions

2 tablespoons chopped fresh cilantro

$\frac{1}{4}$ cup vegetable oil

$\frac{1}{4}$ cup fresh lime juice

1 teaspoon salt

$\frac{1}{8}$ teaspoon black pepper

Calories 133, Total Fat 9g, Carbs 12g, Net Carbs 7g, Fiber 5g, Protein 2g

GAZPACHO SHRIMP SALAD

MAKES 4 SERVINGS

1. Combine salsa, vinegar, oil and garlic in small bowl; mix well.

2. Combine greens, tomato, avocado and cucumber in large bowl. Divide salad among 4 plates; top with shrimp. Drizzle dressing over salads; sprinkle with cilantro.

½ cup chunky salsa

1 tablespoon balsamic vinegar

1 tablespoon extra virgin olive oil

1 clove garlic, minced

8 cups torn mixed salad greens or romaine lettuce

1 large tomato, chopped

1 small ripe avocado, diced

½ cup thinly sliced unpeeled cucumber

8 ounces large cooked shrimp, peeled and deveined

½ cup coarsely chopped fresh cilantro

Calories 190, Total Fat 11g, Carbs 10g, Net Carbs 5g, Fiber 5g, Protein 14g

MAIN-DISH MEDITERRANEAN SALAD

MAKES 4 SERVINGS

1. Place lettuce, green beans, tuna and tomatoes in large bowl.

2. For dressing, whisk oil, vinegar and mustard in small bowl until blended. Season with salt and pepper. Pour dressing over salad; toss well. Serve immediately.

1 package (10 ounces) chopped romaine lettuce

8 ounces fresh green beans, cooked and drained or 1 can (about 14 ounces) whole green beans, drained

1 package ($5^1/_2$ ounces) solid white tuna, flaked

8 ounces cherry tomatoes, halved

2 tablespoons olive oil

2 tablespoons cider vinegar or white vinegar

$1^1/_2$ teaspoons Dijon mustard

Salt and black pepper

Calories 156, Total Fat 8g, Carbs 9g, Net Carbs 5g, Fiber 4g, Protein 13g

WARM STEAK SALAD WITH MUSTARD DRESSING

MAKES 4 SERVINGS

1. Preheat broiler. Position oven rack about 4 inches from heat source.

2. For dressing, whisk oil, rice vinegar, balsamic vinegar, mustard and thyme in medium bowl; season with salt and pepper.

3. Season steak with salt and pepper. Place steak on rack of broiler pan. Broil 13 to 18 minutes for medium rare (145°F) to medium or until desired doneness, turning once.

4. Meanwhile, bring lightly salted water to a boil in medium saucepan. Add snap peas; cook 2 minutes. Drain.

5. Place steak on cutting board. Cut across the grain into thin slices.

6. Line serving platter with lettuce. Arrange steak slices in center of platter. Surround with onion rings, snap peas and cherry tomatoes. Serve with dressing.

3/4 cup olive oil

3 tablespoons seasoned rice vinegar

1 tablespoon balsamic vinegar

1 tablespoon Dijon mustard

1/4 teaspoon dried thyme

Salt and black pepper

1 beef flank steak (about 1 1/4 pounds)

4 ounces sugar snap peas or snow peas

Lettuce leaves

1 medium red onion, sliced and separated into rings

1 pint cherry tomatoes, halved

Calories 620, Total Fat 48g, Carbs 13g, Net Carbs 11g, Fiber 2g, Protein 32g

NOODLE-FREE LASAGNA

MAKES 8 SERVINGS

1. Cut eggplant, zucchini and yellow squash lengthwise into thin (1/8- to 1/4-inch) slices. To reduce excess water, place slices in colander and drain 1 to 2 hours (see Tip).

2. Preheat oven to 375°F. Heat large nonstick skillet over medium-high heat. Add sausage; cook 8 to 10 minutes or until cooked through, stirring to break up meat. Drain fat. Transfer to plate.

3. Add bell peppers and mushrooms to skillet; cook and stir 3 to 4 minutes or until vegetables are tender. Return sausage to skillet. Add tomatoes, tomato sauce, basil, oregano, salt and black pepper; cook and stir 1 to 2 minutes or until heated through.

4. Layer one third of eggplant, zucchini and yellow squash in 13×9-inch baking pan. Spread half of ricotta cheese over vegetables. Top with one third of tomato sauce mixture. Sprinkle evenly with half of mozzarella cheese. Repeat layers once, ending with final layer of vegetables and tomato sauce mixture. Sprinkle with Parmesan cheese; cover with foil.

5. Bake 45 minutes. Remove foil; bake 10 to 15 minutes or until vegetables are tender. Let stand 10 minutes before cutting.

TIP: To reduce excess water from eggplant and squash, place in a colander. Lay a paper towel or clean kitchen towel over the vegetables and weigh them down with a bowl or heavy cans. Let vegetables drain for 1 to 2 hours before preparing recipe. Or bake vegetables 10 minutes in a preheated 350°F oven.

1 medium eggplant

2 medium zucchini

2 medium yellow squash

1 1/4 pounds lean sweet Italian turkey sausage, casings removed

2 medium bell peppers, diced

2 cups mushrooms, thinly sliced

1 can (about 14 ounces) diced tomatoes

1 cup tomato sauce

1/2 cup coarsely chopped fresh basil

1 teaspoon dried oregano

1/2 teaspoon salt

1/4 teaspoon black pepper

1 container (15 ounces) whole-milk ricotta cheese

2 cups (8 ounces) shredded mozzarella cheese

1/4 cup grated Parmesan cheese

Calories 443, Total Fat 34g, Carbs 16g, Net Carbs 9g, Fiber 5g, Protein 24g

SNACKS & TREATS

BACON & ONION CHEESE BALL

MAKES 20 SERVINGS (2 TABLESPOONS PER SERVING)

1. Beat cream cheese, sour cream, bacon bits, $1/2$ cup green onions and blue cheese in large bowl until well blended. Shape mixture into a ball. Wrap in plastic wrap; refrigerate at least 1 hour.

2. Place cheese ball on serving plate. Garnish with additional green onions. Serve with celery and crackers, if desired.

1 package (8 ounces) cream cheese, softened

$1/2$ cup sour cream

$1/2$ cup bottled real bacon bits

$1/2$ cup chopped green onions, plus additional for garnish

$1/4$ cup crumbled blue cheese

Celery sticks and whole wheat crackers (optional)

Calories 77, Total Fat 6g, Carbs 2g, Net Carbs 1g, Fiber 1g, Protein 4g

MUSHROOMS ROCKEFELLER

MAKES 18 APPETIZERS

1. Preheat oven to 375°F. Spray 13×9-inch baking dish with nonstick cooking spray. Brush dirt from mushrooms; clean by wiping mushrooms with damp paper towel. Pull entire stem out of each mushroom cap.

2. Cut thin slice from base of each stem; discard. Chop stems.

3. Cook bacon in medium skillet over medium heat until crisp. Drain bacon on paper towels; set aside. Add mushroom stems and onion to hot drippings in skillet; cook and stir until onion is tender. Add spinach, pimientos, lemon juice and lemon peel; mix well.

4. Stuff mushroom caps with spinach mixture; place in single layer in prepared baking dish. Crumble bacon; sprinkle over tops of mushrooms. Bake 15 minutes or until heated through. Serve immediately.

18 large white mushrooms (about 1 pound)

2 slices bacon

1/4 cup chopped onion

1 package (10 ounces) frozen chopped spinach, thawed and squeezed dry

1 jar (2 ounces) chopped pimientos, drained

1 tablespoon lemon juice

1 teaspoon grated lemon peel

Calories 25, Total Fat 1g, Carbs 2g, Net Carbs 1g, Fiber 1g, Protein 2g

ASPARAGUS FRITTATA PROSCIUTTO CUPS

MAKES 12 CUPS (6 SERVINGS)

1. Preheat oven to 375°F. Spray 12 standard (2½-inch) muffin cups with nonstick cooking spray.

2. Heat oil in large skillet over medium heat. Add onion; cook and stir 4 minutes or until softened. Add asparagus and garlic; cook and stir 8 minutes or until asparagus is crisp-tender. Set aside to cool slightly.

3. Line each prepared muffin cup with prosciutto slice. (Prosciutto should cover cup as much as possible, with edges extending above muffin pan.) Whisk eggs, Cheddar, Parmesan, cream and pepper in large bowl until well blended. Stir in asparagus mixture until blended. Pour into prosciutto-lined cups, filling about three-fourths full.

4. Bake about 20 minutes or until frittatas are puffed and golden brown and edges are pulling away from pan. Cool in pan 10 minutes; remove to wire rack. Serve warm or at room temperature.

1 tablespoon olive oil

1 small red onion, finely chopped

1½ cups sliced asparagus (½-inch pieces)

1 clove garlic, minced

12 thin slices prosciutto

8 eggs

½ cup (2 ounces) shredded white Cheddar cheese

¼ cup grated Parmesan cheese

2 tablespoons whipping cream

⅛ teaspoon black pepper

Calories 270, Total Fat 18g, Carbs 5g, Net Carbs 4g, Fiber 1g, Protein 22g

MINI SPINACH FRITTATAS
MAKES 4 SERVINGS (3 FRITTATAS EACH)

1. Preheat oven to 350°F. Spray 12 standard (2½-inch) muffin cups with nonstick cooking spray.

2. Heat oil in large nonstick skillet over medium heat. Add onion; cook and stir about 5 minutes or until tender. Set aside to cool slightly.

3. Whisk eggs and yogurt in large bowl. Stir in spinach, Cheddar, Parmesan, salt, black pepper, red pepper, nutmeg and onion until blended. Divide mixture evenly among prepared muffin cups.

4. Bake 20 to 25 minutes or until eggs are puffed and firm and no longer shiny. Cool in pan 2 minutes. Loosen bottom and sides with small spatula or knife; remove to wire rack. Serve warm, cold or at room temperature.

1 tablespoon olive oil

½ cup chopped onion

8 eggs

¼ cup plain yogurt

1 package (10 ounces) frozen chopped spinach, thawed and squeezed dry

½ cup (2 ounces) shredded white Cheddar cheese

¼ cup grated Parmesan cheese

¾ teaspoon salt

⅛ teaspoon black pepper

⅛ teaspoon ground red pepper

Dash ground nutmeg

Calories 290, Total Fat 20g, Carbs 6g, Net Carbs 4g, Fiber 2g, Protein 21g

BLT CUKES
MAKES 8 TO 10 PIECES

1. Combine lettuce, spinach, bacon, tomato, mayonnaise, pepper and salt in medium bowl; mix well.

2. Peel cucumber; trim off ends and cut in half lengthwise. Use spoon to scoop out seeds; discard seeds.

3. Divide bacon mixture between cucumber halves, mounding in center. Sprinkle with green onion. Cut into 2-inch pieces.

TIP: These snacks can be made, covered and refrigerated up to 12 hours ahead of time.

$\frac{1}{2}$ cup finely chopped lettuce

$\frac{1}{2}$ cup finely chopped baby spinach

3 slices bacon, crisp-cooked and crumbled

$\frac{1}{4}$ cup finely diced tomato

$1\frac{1}{2}$ tablespoons mayonnaise

$\frac{1}{4}$ teaspoon black pepper

$\frac{1}{8}$ teaspoon salt

1 large cucumber

Minced green onion (optional)

Calories 26, Total Fat 3g, Carbs 2g, Net Carbs 1g, Fiber 1g, Protein 2g

ASPARAGUS AND HAM BUNDLES

MAKES 6 SERVINGS

1. Preheat oven to 350°F. Place asparagus on baking sheet. Drizzle with oil and sprinkle with salt and pepper. Roast about 10 minutes or until crisp-tender; keep warm.

2. Heat small nonstick skillet over medium heat. Add 1 tablespoon green onion; cook and stir 10 seconds. Beat 1 egg in small bowl; add to skillet, allowing to spread in circle. *Do not stir.* Place ham slice on top of egg crêpe; cook until heated through. Remove from skillet. Repeat with remaining green onion, eggs and ham.

3. Place 2 asparagus spears on each crêpe; roll up. Tie each bundle with reserved green onion tops. Serve immediately.

VARIATION: Top ham with shredded Swiss cheese.

12 asparagus spears

1 tablespoon olive oil

Salt and black pepper

6 green onions, white part diced and green tops reserved

6 eggs

6 slices boiled ham

Calories 124, Total Fat 8g, Carbs 2g, Net Carbs 1g, Fiber 1g, Protein 11g

STUFFED MUSHROOM CAPS

MAKES 4 SERVINGS (6 MUSHROOMS EACH)

1. Preheat oven to 350°F. Remove stems from mushrooms and finely chop. Spray baking sheet with nonstick cooking spray.

2. Melt butter in medium skillet over medium-high heat. Add chopped mushrooms; cook and stir 5 minutes. Add chicken, Parmesan cheese, basil, lemon juice, onion powder, salt, garlic powder and pepper; cook and stir 5 minutes. Remove from heat; stir in cream cheese.

3. Spoon mixture into mushroom caps; place on prepared baking sheet. Bake 10 to 15 minutes or until heated through. Sprinkle with paprika.

- 2 packages (8 ounces each) whole mushrooms
- 1 tablespoon butter
- 2/3 cup finely chopped cooked chicken
- 1/4 cup grated Parmesan cheese
- 1 tablespoon chopped fresh basil
- 2 teaspoons lemon juice
- 1/8 teaspoon onion powder
- 1/8 teaspoon salt
- Pinch garlic powder
- Pinch black pepper
- 3 ounces cream cheese, softened
- Paprika

Calories 180, Total Fat 12g, Carbs 5g, Net Carbs 4g, Fiber 1g, Protein 13g

BAGNA CAUDA

MAKES 10 SERVINGS

SLOW COOKER DIRECTIONS

1. Combine oil, butter, anchovies, garlic and red pepper flakes in food processor; process until smooth. Transfer to small slow cooker.

2. Cover; cook on LOW 2 hours or on HIGH 1 hour or until mixture is heated through. Turn slow cooker to LOW or WARM. Serve with assorted dippers.

TIP: Bagna cauda is a warm Italian dip similar to fondue. The name means "warm bath" in Italian.

$3/4$ cup olive oil

6 tablespoons butter, softened

12 anchovy fillets, drained

6 cloves garlic, peeled

$1/8$ teaspoon red pepper flakes

Assorted dippers: endive spears, cauliflower florets, cucumber spears, carrot sticks, zucchini spears, red bell pepper strips and/or sugar snap peas

Calories 220, Total Fat 24g, Carbs 1g, Net Carbs 1g, Fiber 0g, Protein 2g

CRAB CANAPÉS
MAKES 16 SERVINGS

1. Combine cream cheese, lemon juice and hot pepper sauce in medium bowl; mix well. Stir in crabmeat, bell pepper and green onions. Cover and refrigerate at least 1 hour to allow flavors to blend.

2. When ready to serve, spoon $1\frac{1}{2}$ teaspoons crabmeat mixture onto each cucumber slice. Garnish with parsley.

$\frac{2}{3}$ cup cream cheese, softened

2 teaspoons lemon juice

1 teaspoon hot pepper sauce

1 package (8 ounces) imitation crabmeat or lobster, flaked

$\frac{1}{3}$ cup chopped red bell pepper

2 green onions, sliced (about $\frac{1}{4}$ cup)

64 cucumber slices (about $2\frac{1}{2}$ medium cucumbers cut into $\frac{3}{8}$-inch-thick slices)

Chopped fresh parsley (optional)

Calories 51, Total Fat 4g, Carbs 4g, Net Carbs 3g, Fiber 1g, Protein 4g

SMOKED SALMON OMELET ROLL-UPS

MAKES 6 SERVINGS (4 PIECES EACH)

1. Whisk eggs and pepper in small bowl until well blended (no streaks of white showing). Spray large nonstick skillet with nonstick cooking spray; heat over medium-high heat.

2. Pour half of egg mixture into skillet; tilt skillet to completely coat bottom with thin layer of eggs. Cook without stirring 2 to 4 minutes or until eggs are set. Use spatula to carefully loosen omelet from skillet; slide onto cutting board. Repeat with remaining egg mixture to make second omelet.

3. Spread 2 tablespoons cream cheese over each omelet; top with smoked salmon pieces. Roll up omelets tightly; wrap in plastic wrap and refrigerate at least 30 minutes. Cut off ends, then cut rolls crosswise into $1/2$-inch slices.

4 eggs

$1/8$ teaspoon black pepper

$1/4$ cup cream cheese, softened

1 package (about 4 ounces) smoked salmon, cut into bite-size pieces

Calories 100, Total Fat 5g, Carbs 1g, Net Carbs 1g, Fiber 0g, Protein 14g

BACON AND CHEESE DIP

MAKES 16 SERVINGS (¼ CUP EACH)

SLOW COOKER DIRECTIONS

1. Combine cream cheese, Colby-Jack cheese, cream, mustard, onion, Worcestershire sauce, salt and hot pepper sauce in small slow cooker.

2. Cover; cook on LOW 1 hour or until cheese melts, stirring occasionally.

3. Stir in bacon; adjust seasonings. Serve with vegetable dippers.

2 packages (8 ounces each) cream cheese, cut into cubes

4 cups (16 ounces) shredded Colby-Jack cheese

1 cup whipping cream

2 tablespoons prepared mustard

1 tablespoon minced onion

2 teaspoons Worcestershire sauce

½ teaspoon salt

¼ teaspoon hot pepper sauce

1 pound bacon, crisp-cooked and crumbled

Vegetables for dipping

Calories 360, Total Fat 29g, Carbs 3g, Net Carbs 3g, Fiber 0g, Protein 20g

PICANTE VEGETABLE DIP

MAKES 13 SERVINGS (2 TABLESPOONS EACH)

1. Combine sour cream, picante sauce, mayonnaise, bell pepper, green onion and garlic salt in medium bowl until well blended.

2. Cover; refrigerate several hours or overnight to allow flavors to blend. Serve with dippers.

$^2/_3$ cup sour cream

$^1/_2$ cup picante sauce

$^1/_3$ cup mayonnaise

$^1/_4$ cup finely chopped green or red bell pepper

2 tablespoons finely chopped green onion

$^3/_4$ teaspoon garlic salt

Vegetables for dipping

Calories 61, Total Fat 6g, Carbs 2g, Net Carbs 1g, Fiber 1g, Protein 1g

LOX BITES

MAKES 10 SERVINGS (3 BITES EACH)

1. Cut ends off of cucumbers; cut each cucumber into 10 slices. Scoop out cucumber slices with a rounded $1/2$ teaspoon, leaving thin shell.

2. Combine onion, cream cheese, 1 tablespoon chives, lemon juice and horseradish sauce in small bowl; mix well. Stir in salmon.

3. Spoon about 1 tablespoon salmon mixture into each cucumber cup. Garnish with additional chives. Serve immediately.

NOTE: Take the classic combination of lox, bagels and cream cheese and turn it into a light and fresh appetizer. Lox is smoked salmon that has been brine-cured before smoking, resulting in a saltier taste.

3 English cucumbers, peeled

3 tablespoons finely chopped red onion

2 tablespoons cream cheese, softened

1 tablespoon chopped fresh chives, plus additional for garnish

1 tablespoon fresh lemon juice

1 tablespoon horseradish sauce

8 ounces smoked salmon, coarsely chopped

Calories 55, Total Fat 2g, Carbs 4g, Net Carbs 3g, Fiber 1g, Protein 5g

METRIC CONVERSION CHART

VOLUME MEASUREMENTS (dry)

1/8 teaspoon = 0.5 mL
1/4 teaspoon = 1 mL
1/2 teaspoon = 2 mL
3/4 teaspoon = 4 mL
1 teaspoon = 5 mL
1 tablespoon = 15 mL
2 tablespoons = 30 mL
1/4 cup = 60 mL
1/3 cup = 75 mL
1/2 cup = 125 mL
2/3 cup = 150 mL
3/4 cup = 175 mL
1 cup = 250 mL
2 cups = 1 pint = 500 mL
3 cups = 750 mL
4 cups = 1 quart = 1 L

VOLUME MEASUREMENTS (fluid)

1 fluid ounce (2 tablespoons) = 30 mL
4 fluid ounces (1/2 cup) = 125 mL
8 fluid ounces (1 cup) = 250 mL
12 fluid ounces (1 1/2 cups) = 375 mL
16 fluid ounces (2 cups) = 500 mL

WEIGHTS (mass)

1/2 ounce = 15 g
1 ounce = 30 g
3 ounces = 90 g
4 ounces = 120 g
8 ounces = 225 g
10 ounces = 285 g
12 ounces = 360 g
16 ounces = 1 pound = 450 g

DIMENSIONS

1/16 inch = 2 mm
1/8 inch = 3 mm
1/4 inch = 6 mm
1/2 inch = 1.5 cm
3/4 inch = 2 cm
1 inch = 2.5 cm

OVEN TEMPERATURES

250°F = 120°C
275°F = 140°C
300°F = 150°C
325°F = 160°C
350°F = 180°C
375°F = 190°C
400°F = 200°C
425°F = 220°C
450°F = 230°C

BAKING PAN SIZES

Utensil	Size in Inches/Quarts	Metric Volume	Size in Centimeters
Baking or	8×8×2	2 L	20×20×5
Cake Pan	9×9×2	2.5 L	23×23×5
(square or	12×8×2	3 L	30×20×5
rectangular)	13×9×2	3.5 L	33×23×5
Loaf Pan	8×4×3	1.5 L	20×10×7
	9×5×3	2 L	23×13×7
Round Layer	8×1½	1.2 L	20×4
Cake Pan	9×1½	1.5 L	23×4
Pie Plate	8×1¼	750 mL	20×3
	9×1¼	1 L	23×3
Baking Dish	1 quart	1 L	—
or Casserole	1½ quart	1.5 L	—
	2 quart	2 L	—